KEPT FOR A PURPOSE

A True Story of Peril, Forgiveness, and Unexpected Favor

KEPT FOR A PURPOSE

A True Story of Peril, Forgiveness, and Unexpected Favor

Jean Bosco G.
with Karen Panton WalkingEagle

HAVENDALE PRESS

HAVENDALE PRESS

www.havendalepress.com

Cover and Interior Design: Cathy Richmond Robinson

ISBN: 978-1-7372509-2-0 (paperback)

To my wife, Everlyn,
my children, Isabellah and Ivan,
and followers of Jesus Christ
around the world.

Praise for *Kept for a Purpose*

"This book is equal parts adventure and inspiration. As an educator, I especially welcome this literary work because it serves as an introduction to a historical event that too few Americans know anything about. Told through the eyes of a teenager, it should be on the reading list of every serious student of history and the social sciences, regardless of age. But Bosco's story does more than captivate and educate. It will light a spark of hope and encouragement within the heart and mind of every teenager and adult who reads it."

—Sandra Reid,
Maryland High School Principal of the Year (2017)

"Reverend Bosco's miraculous escape from the genocide in Rwanda will reinforce your faith in the mighty power of God to provide for his children and to protect them in the worst of circumstances. His powerful true story is a testimony to the fact that when God is with you, there is no telling how far you can go."

—Reverend Juliet Mahugu, senior pastor,
Christ Is The Answer Ministries, Woodley, Kenya

"Reverend Bosco's life clearly communicates the inescapable truth: nothing in this world can separate us from the love of God that is in Christ Jesus our Lord."

—Reverend Ananie Nduwamungu,
PCEA St. Andrew's Church, Nairobi

"As a professor of political science, I had studied and taught college students about the historical, social, cultural, economic, and political forces that shaped and influenced the one hundred days of terror that engulfed Rwanda in 1994. But while I was familiar with the genocide that had unfolded, my knowledge was academic and therefore incomplete. *Kept for a Purpose* transported me to places that textbooks could not. It engaged not only my mind but also my emotions. Bosco's deeply personal and ultimately inspiring account of that dreadful period will hopefully raise questions and stimulate valuable discussions in universities, high schools, and around kitchen tables."

—**Winsome A. Downie**, PhD, Department of Political Science, Manhattan College, Bronx, New York

"Through his amazing life story, Reverend Bosco teaches valuable lessons about love, forgiveness, heavenly provision, and the blessings that are available to all who answer God's call. Read, then pass it on so that someone else may also be blessed."

—**Reverend Jesse Mwai**, senior pastor, Christ Is The Answer Ministries, Buruburu, Kenya

"*Kept for a Purpose* is a wonderful book. Your life will be richer for having read this true and encouraging story of how good triumphed over evil."

—**Reverend Ken Kimiywe**, former deputy bishop, Christ Is The Answer Ministries (CITAM), and senior pastor, CITAM Thika Road, Kenya

Table of Contents

Foreword   What God Intends by Richard Stearns   xv
Introduction   1

PART ONE: **Innocence**   **5**

Chapter 1   Firstborn Son   7
Chapter 2   Little Boss Man   15
Chapter 3   Sowing the Seeds   21
Chapter 4   Growing Unrest   29

PART TWO: **Things Fall Apart**   **41**

Chapter 5   Death on the Doorstep   43
Chapter 6   No Way Out   53
Chapter 7   Enemies All Around   63
Chapter 8   Through the Forest   71

PART THREE: **No Longer Alone**   **79**

Chapter 9   Exodus   81
Chapter 10   Road to Zaire   91
Chapter 11   The Four Laws   101
Chapter 12   A New Beginning   113

PART FOUR: Unexpected Favor   **125**

Chapter 13   Into the Dark   127
Chapter 14   The Crossing   139
Chapter 15   Angel along the Way   151

PART FIVE: Promises Fulfilled   **161**

Chapter 16   Miracles   163
Chapter 17   Lost No More   177
Chapter 18   Destiny Revealed   189

Epilogue   201
Acknowledgements   205
Notes   207
About the Authors   209

Author's Note

In telling my story, I have changed the names of many individuals. Almost thirty years have passed since this most traumatic period in my life, and I simply cannot recall their actual names. In a few cases, I have changed names intentionally to protect identities. Similarly, because I am unable to recall precise dates, I have estimated the time frames within which certain incidents occurred. As is common in works of memoir, the conversations I narrate may not always reflect the exact words that were said at the time of these events. However, they do accurately convey the essence of exchanges I had with individuals, as well as conversations between others for which I was present.

Fear not, for I am with you; be not dismayed, for I am your God. I will strengthen you, yes, I will help you, I will uphold you with my righteous right hand.

—Isaiah 41:10 (NLT)

Foreword

What God Intends

By Richard Stearns

I n my former role as president of World Vision US, I traveled to
Rwanda on several occasions. During some of these visits, I spoke
with people who had experienced the horror of the 1994 genocide
firsthand. I have also read many of the news reports, books, journals,
and magazines that detail events during that period and in the difficult
months and years that followed. Undoubtedly Rwanda was one of the
bleakest places on earth during those one hundred days when almost
one million people were killed.

The true story you are about to read takes place during that terrible
period in Rwanda; however, it is unique in that it inspires both hope
and faith. Unlike so many other books about the genocide, this story
is told through the eyes of a child. The author, Jean Bosco, was only
fourteen years old when he was thrust into the mayhem and madness
that overtook his country. He was the son of a Tutsi mother and a
Hutu father, which made his situation particularly precarious. While
his father's Hutu heritage offered some protection from the ethnic
violence that consumed his country, his mother's Tutsi heritage, which

manifested itself quite visibly in Bosco's facial features, placed him in grave danger from those who sought to execute the Tutsis and remove them from the land forever. In an ethnic conflict that compelled Hutu to side with Hutu and Tutsi with Tutsi, he found himself in a no-man's-land, vulnerable, terrified, and confused.

Bosco's story, with its unexpected twists and turns, will captivate your imagination and stir your emotions. But for many, it will be his amazing spiritual journey during this tumultuous period that will leave the most indelible mark. Unlike those who were crushed by the weight of both a national and personal disaster, this teenager experienced an amazing transformation in mind and spirit—a transformation he credits with saving his life and helping him find his purpose. It is a transformation that, given the context within which it occurred, can only be described as miraculous.

In the months leading up to April 1994, ethnic hatred had been aggressively stoked by political leaders and the media. And so when the figurative "match" was lit by the assassination of the Rwandan president, the economic, social, ethnic, and political tensions that had been simmering erupted into a mighty fireball of violence. The result? Mass murder of stranger by stranger, neighbor by neighbor, coworker by coworker, student by student, even friend by friend.

People often ask, "How could that have happened?" This question is sometimes followed by another: "Could that ever happen here?" Americans invariably respond with a swift and confident "No!" But as I reflect on these questions, I am forced to conclude that the *potential* for this kind of violence exists within the heart of every person, community, and country. Rwandans are not unique. What they did to each other is what the people of every country, including America, are capable of doing also.

Rwanda should therefore serve as a warning and an example of what can happen if we demonize whole groups of people in our society and paint them with a broad brush of negative stereotypes and disparaging labels. And if we seek a wider audience for our vitriol by harnessing the media and the internet to spread our brand of hate, the potential for nationwide violence increases dramatically. Recall that many in Rwanda used the media, especially radio, in precisely this way.

But God. I savor those words because of the hope they offer. They signify that no matter how terrible the situation, our Lord can intervene and turn things around. This assures me that what happened in Rwanda is by no means inevitable. Hate does not necessarily win even when it looks like it will. The Bible reminds us that situations can change for the better in the most unexpected ways. The story of Joseph aptly illustrates this. Joseph was sold into slavery in Egypt and was falsely accused and imprisoned for many years. Ultimately, however, the Pharaoh freed Joseph and promoted him. He became the highest-ranking official in the Pharaoh's palace, where he made wise decisions that helped avert famine and starvation in the land. Because of his position, he was able to save the lives of many, including his brothers who had sold him into slavery years before. Reflecting on how he had come to be where he was at just the right time, Joseph concluded, "You intended to harm me, *but God* intended it all for good."

But God. Those words also help explain how Bosco emerged from an experience that could have doomed him and fueled hatred and anger toward those who harmed him and his family for a lifetime. But God used several people to intervene in his circumstances in the most remarkable ways. As a result, today Bosco is a faithful servant of God who teaches others about grace, forgiveness, and the path to reconciliation.

What happened in Rwanda never needs to happen elsewhere in the world, even if internal conflicts and strife currently exist. Similarly, children around the globe who are currently mired in poverty, war, or other dire circumstances are not destined to live hopeless, unfulfilled lives. You and I can make the difference if we choose to be used by God to counter speech that stirs up anger, feeds hate, and spreads lies. If we choose to be the hands that heal divisions and the lips that speak the truth. If we choose to love and support children like Bosco. If we help them to grow up whole and healed from past trauma. If we are prepared to share our faith, the most powerful antidote to all that is wicked. If we are willing to be used in *But God* moments to help turn around the lives of those going in the wrong direction. Because when we show people the love of Christ, we draw them to the cross of Christ.

Indeed, we can be the peacemakers whom Jesus mentioned in his Sermon on the Mount. He said they will be blessed and will be called "sons of God." What an honor! But to be the kind of peacemakers who can help prevent violence from spiraling out of control in our communities, we must, as Bosco did, become rooted in our faith. To promote relationships and mutual understanding and to help others discover and experience the future God intended for them, our speech and deeds must reflect that faith. We must be prepared to lend a helping hand to people in need—people like young Bosco.

Without the peacemakers in his life who resembled Jesus, the ones who comforted him, protected him, provided for him, and shared the gospel with him, Bosco's deeply personal story of deliverance could never have been told. Without those who were willing to build bridges to opportunities for him when he had little more than the clothes on his back, his riveting testament—to the power of Jesus to transform lives and to the ability of love and generosity to defeat evil—might never have been written. But thankfully it was, and we are blessed by it.

Richard Stearns is president emeritus of World Vision US. He is also the best-selling author of *The Hole in Our Gospel* and *Lead Like it Matters to God: Values-Driven Leadership in a Success-Driven World.*

Introduction

I don't remember which came first. Was it the rapid burst of automatic rifle fire or the first exploding grenade? Sheer terror overwhelmed me. "Turn around, turn around!" The large man whom my father had sent to get me screamed instructions at our driver, Jacques. Moments before Jacques had slammed on the brakes, an instinctive act that saved our lives as a second grenade exploded in the road just a few meters in front of us. But we were still in danger. I could see gravel flying into the air as a fresh hail of bullets from the hills rained down on us and collided with the ground around our jeep.

Still in danger. At the time I had no idea how accurate that assessment of my situation really was. It was April 1994. Only fourteen years old, I was being sucked up into a powerful tornado of death and disruption in Rwanda's capital city of Kigali, and I was in shock. I did not know then that the tumultuous whirlwinds would not subside for three long years.

Rwanda is the fourth-smallest country in Africa. At just over twenty-six thousand square kilometers, it is comparable in size to the American state of Maryland, where I now live with my wife and two children. I can still see the stunning beauty of my homeland, located in the Great Rift Valley region, at the point where central and eastern Africa converge. Bordered by Uganda to the north, the Democratic Republic of

1

the Congo to the west, Burundi to the south, and Tanzania to the east, Rwanda boasts spectacular mountain ranges along its western margin, where dense tropical forests and terraced farmlands cover steep volcanic cones. Rolling hills and valleys give way to rivers and lakes scattered throughout the lower-lying grasslands to the east. Kigali sits near the center of the country. The country's two largest ethnic groups, Hutus and Tutsis, are culturally the same—they speak the same language, live together within the same communities, and follow the same traditions. Intermarriage is common, and over the years it has become increasingly difficult to distinguish between ethnic Hutus and ethnic Tutsis. Generally speaking, however, the Tutsis are lighter-skinned, taller, slimmer, and have narrower noses than the darker, shorter, and more muscular Hutus.

Rwanda was first colonized by the Germans in the 1800s and then by the Belgians in the early 1900s. When Belgian colonists initially arrived, they introduced a system of classifying people according to their ethnicity and required all Rwandans to carry ethnic identification cards. But not only did the Belgians draw an ethnic distinction between Rwandans, for many years they also treated the minority, Tutsis, more favorably than the majority, Hutus. By treating the Tutsis as superior and giving them access to better economic and educational opportunities, the Belgians stirred up resentment among the Hutus toward the Tutsis. This simmering animosity would periodically boil over into violent attacks by Hutus against Tutsis.

When Rwanda became an independent nation in 1962, the majority Hutus ascended to power. In the decades that followed, the frequency and intensity of the violence against the Tutsis increased, and large numbers of Tutsis were killed or forced to flee to neighboring countries such as Burundi, Tanzania, and Uganda. For a variety of social, political, and economic reasons that are beyond the scope of this book, animosity toward the Tutsis escalated throughout the early 1990s. Then, on April 6, 1994, the president of Rwanda, Juvénal Habyarimana, a Hutu, was killed along with several others when his plane was shot down near the airport in Kigali.

Some believe that Habyarimana was murdered by Hutu extremists within his own government who viewed him as too moderate and opposed his efforts to work with the Tutsis. Others blamed the Tutsis for shooting down the president's plane. Regardless of who was responsible, the response to the president's death was swift and violent. A nationwide slaughter of Tutsis began. Moderate Hutus, both private citizens and government officials, who sought to protect Tutsis or who had expressed a willingness to share political power with the Tutsis were also killed by more extremist Hutus, who wanted to rid the entire country of all Tutsis. By the time the genocide ended three months later, close to one million Rwandans were dead.

I share this very brief history of Rwanda because it is important for you to understand if you are to make sense of the events described in this book. Everything that happened to me between 1994 and 1997 was the direct result of the Rwandan genocide and later the First Congo War, which began around October 1996. As the name suggests, the latter took place in the Democratic Republic of the Congo, which at the time was still known as Zaire.

Both the genocide and the war had far-reaching human, economic, and political consequences, both locally and internationally; however, this book is not a political or historical text. It is the true account of what happened to me when I was a teenager during those years. I had a limited understanding of the chaos that was unfolding around me, and I struggled greatly to make sense of the senselessness. Survival, not politics, was all that mattered to me.

I experienced intense pain and suffering during this three-year period. So extreme was my distress at times that, had I known the magnitude of the anguish I was about to endure, I may have welcomed death that day when those unknown assailants aimed grenades and automatic rifle fire at my traveling companions and me. Yet my story is one of spiritual awakening, forgiveness, and overcoming. That is what I choose to celebrate in this book. After all that I lived through, I can confidently attest that in the midst of trauma, the miraculous can happen, and God's grace can abound.

Against all odds I survived. Survived and completed my college degree. Survived and became a pastor who would, years later, move with my family to the United States to lead a church in Maryland. Most importantly, I survived to fulfill a fervent promise I had whispered to Jesus when as a teenager I languished in a hot and dusty refugee camp. "If you get me out of here, I will serve you the rest of my life," I had prayed. This is the story of how I endured the storm—a personal testimony of how I was upheld by my Lord's righteous right hand and kept for his divine purpose—and was eventually able to live out that humble promise.

PART ONE
Innocence

CHAPTER 1
Firstborn Son

My heart was pounding and the tendons in my skinny legs strained to the point of almost tearing. *Only a few more meters to go*, I told myself. But the dogs were ferocious and fast. Was that the hot breath of the large brown one on my calf? I dared not look behind and find out for sure. "Run faster, Bosco, run!" My friend Florentin had already cleared the wall that would separate us from the dogs and was now yelling to me from the other side. Paul, who sat directly behind me in class, had just reached the wall and was frantically pulling himself up to the top. Only I remained on the wrong side of the wall, and the dogs were gaining on me.

It was not surprising that I would be last in this sprint to safety. I was almost a year younger than many of my classmates, and I struggled to keep up both academically and athletically. My father had thought it a good idea for me to start school earlier than everyone else because he feared that if I was idle at home, I might get myself into trouble. That would bring shame to the family. Avoiding family shame was one of his biggest concerns, and he often warned me against it. Now it dawned on me that I might be torn to pieces by the dogs because I was slower than the other boys in grade five. That would *definitely* cause Papa to feel ashamed.

A few strides later, I reached the wall. As I scrambled to hoist myself beyond the reach of the dogs' fangs, a pair of hands grabbed the collar of my shirt and pulled me up and over. Seconds later Paul and I collapsed in the grass at Florentin's feet. The three of us laughed loudly in relief but not loud enough to drown out the barking dogs or the threats hurled by the watchman on the other side of the wall. "If you boys come back into this yard again, I will make sure the dogs take care of you," he shouted angrily.

Though it was risky, this was not the first time we had climbed into this specific yard. The passion fruit that grew there was sweet, and we looked forward to filling our pockets with the tasty treat every couple of weeks. I also enjoyed the rush of adrenaline I experienced during these escapades. My father had made it clear on multiple occasions that I was to come home directly after school every day, but like many twelve-year-old boys, I sometimes felt the need to challenge parental authority. I was not brave enough to do so openly—my father would not have tolerated blatant defiance—so I had to be satisfied with secret acts of rebellion like roaming with Florentin and Paul after school and stealing fruit from our neighbors' trees.

I was the firstborn son and third child of my father, Michel Gapfizi, and my mother, Vivian. Born in 1979, I had been given the name Jean Bosco Gapfizi; however, only my passport and other official documents listed my official last name. On formal occasions when both a first and last name were required, I preferred to be called Jean Bosco, and among most of my friends and family, I was known simply as Bosco. This was ironic because as the oldest son, I was the only one of my siblings to be given my father's last name at birth. My sisters and brothers were all given their own unique last names, as was the custom in Rwanda.

When I was about seven or eight years old, we moved from Gikomero, where my two older sisters and I were born, to Nyakabanda, which was much closer to the center of the capital city of Kigali. Our house was built on Mont Kigali, a hill overlooking the downtown area, as well as the international airport. My three sisters, two brothers, and I enjoyed watching the planes take off and land in the distance through the large windows in our living room. Home was a happy and comfortable place. My parents and siblings loved me and each other. We had everything we needed and much of what we wanted.

I was especially close to my two older sisters. Born in 1977 and 1978, respectively, Francoise and Marie-Jeanne were also my best friends, and we laughed together quite a bit. They both had the tendency to be overprotective, keeping a watchful eye on me as we walked down the street to catch the bus to school in the mornings and being as attentive to my appearance as to their own. They would insist that my mother buy only the most fashionable clothes for me, and they took personal responsibility for ensuring that I looked my best whenever we went out. Whatever I asked of them, they would usually do without fussing with me the way my younger sister Claudine would.

Although I knew Francoise and Marie-Jeanne felt genuine affection for me, I was keenly aware of the other reason they were so accommodating. As teenagers, my sisters grew increasingly attractive, and many boys at school noticed. I became their secret courier. They relied on me to carry notes and messages between them and the boys they liked best. If my parents had learned about these secret letters, my sisters would have been in big trouble, but Francoise and Marie-Jeanne knew there was nothing to fear with me in charge of communications. It was our secret, and it made our bond even stronger.

In stark contrast Claudine and I argued incessantly. I was only a year older, and she resented my attempts to exercise my authority. She was also extremely competitive and would become frustrated when I got the better of her when we played soccer or other games in our yard. My younger brothers, Twahirwa and Niyitegeka, were less inclined to quarrel with me. When my parents were away from home, I would try to play the role of the boss, but Twahirwa, who was three years my junior, would simply ignore my instructions. Niyitegeka, the youngest in the family, was perhaps the only one of my siblings who was more amused than annoyed by my antics.

My domineering behavior toward my younger siblings aside, we all enjoyed a comfortable and untroubled life within our compound, as our large house and the spacious gardens that surrounded it were called. Similar in size to the other compounds on our street, our main house had two living rooms, one for adults and one for children. My parents had many friends, and on weekends we would often visit each other's homes. While the adults were socializing in the larger of the two living rooms, the children would go to the smaller room to play and talk. My mother had furnished this room with smaller tables and chairs to make clear that this was our own space.

Toward the back of the house was a formal dining room, which held a long glass cabinet used to store the plates and glasses for entertaining guests. An assortment of alcoholic drinks and sodas was also stowed there. Next to the dining room was our ceremonial kitchen. Christophe, who was in charge of preparing and serving our meals, did not actually cook our food in the ceremonial kitchen. Rather, he used it as a staging area to move the food from pots into large serving dishes, which he would then bring to us in the dining room. In a smaller building behind the house was the main kitchen, where Christophe did the cooking.

To the left of the dining room were a bathroom, my bedroom, my parents' bedroom, and a guest bedroom. To the right were three other bedrooms that my five siblings shared and a second bathroom. The seventh bedroom was in the back, away from the other rooms. It had its own entrance that opened directly onto the yard. My older cousin Thomas had moved into that bedroom when I was in elementary school. Thomas was in college studying to become a mechanical engineer, and my father helped to support him financially. He also worked in my father's wholesale and retail businesses during summer vacations.

Along with the working kitchen, the building behind our house included additional bedrooms where Christophe, Chantal, our housekeeper, and Francois, who helped manage my father's business, lived. Detached from this building but only a few steps away was another small structure that housed the third bathroom. Everyone used this bathroom during the day. At nights my family used the bathrooms inside the main house.

A variety of fruit trees grew in our front yard. They were separated from a large vegetable garden by the long driveway that extended from the main gate to a garage near our front door. Our watchman, Victor, tended the fruit and vegetable gardens, as well as the lawn. He also opened and closed the gate for my parents as they drove in and out throughout the day. He did all this while keeping an eye on the gate and the imposing wall around our three-acre property to ensure no one entered the compound without the express permission of my parents.

Victor had a bed in the garage where he slept on the nights that he did not go home to his family, who lived nearby. In one corner of the compound, he had created a small makeshift structure out of wooden planks. This was his own private "kitchen," where he would cook vegetable stews and other simple dishes over an open fire. A small shed next to the gate sheltered him when it rained. Outside the front wall was a line of trees that helped to create an attractive barrier between our property and the street. The trees also contributed to the quiet and secluded atmosphere of our home. Beyond the wall a paved road ran past several other compounds. As with our home, only the roofs of our neighbors' houses were visible from the street.

My parents insisted that my siblings and I behave well and dress properly at all times but especially when we walked through our front gate. Perhaps because I was the oldest boy and carried my father's name, their expectations were high for me. "You must not spoil this boy," Papa would say to Maman. "We cannot allow him to go wherever he wants and spend time with whomever he chooses. If we are not careful, he will be led astray by those boys on the street, and before you know it, he will bring shame on our family!"

Once, when I asked Papa if I could play soccer with my classmates after school, his response was firm and swift. "Why do you want to get dirty and sweaty playing out there?" he scolded. "If your clothes get torn and people see you on the street looking disheveled, what will they think? Do you want to embarrass me in front of my friends?" But a few days later, he came home with a new soccer ball. "Here," he said, handing it to me. "Now you can play as much soccer as you want to with your sisters and brothers at home." Maman assured me that Papa was simply worried about my safety. "He is afraid you might break your leg or learn bad habits from those other children," she explained with a gentle smile. Because of Papa's strict rules, I rarely went beyond the walls of the compound without one or both of my parents. School was the only exception.

It was at the beginning of fifth grade that Florentin told me about the shortcut. We were just leaving school when he pulled me aside.

"Hey! Come with me, Bosco; I want to show you something."

"I can't," I protested. "I'll miss the bus."

Several of my classmates were standing around the bus stop ready to board the bus, which I could see approaching in the distance.

"Don't worry," Florentin insisted as he grabbed my arm. "I promise you will get home before the bus even gets to your street."

Reluctantly I allowed Florentin to lead me down several streets and unpaved paths, and before I realized it, we were standing only a few blocks from my house. It was an amazing discovery! Florentin's shortcut is how I was able to carve out a small window of time each week to get into the kind of mischief that Papa feared. My friends and I were familiar with the circuitous route that the bus took, as well as traffic patterns in the city. This helped us to figure out how much time we could spend climbing walls and picking fruit from the trees of neighboring compounds while still managing to get to the bus stop near my house before the bus arrived. Some days we would skip the fruit in favor of a quick soccer game on a nearby field. I relished the freedom and independence that the shortcut afforded, even as I was careful not to soil or tear my clothes. When the bus pulled up to the corner, I was always there to meet it. I would then casually merge with the other students as they disembarked and make the short walk with them to our respective homes. My parents assumed I had taken the bus all the way home from school, and I was secretly proud of myself for outsmarting Papa in this way.

Later, after the genocide began, other thoughts that were far more important than outwitting Papa would consume me. I would often think, for example, about the sense of security that our money, watchman, locked gates, and walled compound created. Yet our vulnerability would be laid bare so easily. If our wealth and status could not protect us, I would often ask myself, in what or whom could I reasonably trust?

CHAPTER 2
Little Boss Man

"Let's go, Bosco. Do not make me late." I opened my eyes to find Papa standing at the foot of my bed. He was already dressed for work, his crisp white shirt hugging his broad shoulders and thick upper arms tightly, his Afro combed and perfectly round; not a hair was out of place. As he turned to leave, the faint scent of soap lingered in the air.

It was the first day of summer vacation, and all I wanted to do was sleep a little longer. But Papa had other plans for me. Intent on teaching me the value of hard work, self-reliance, discipline, and responsibility, he had decided that the best way to accomplish all of that was for me to go to work in his business. Papa disapproved of the way my older sisters and mother catered to me. He was right—they did spoil me, and yes, I did enjoy their attention and affection. To counter the negative effects of this pampering, Papa insisted that I work in his wholesale store during the school holidays. I remember when he first made the announcement. "You are almost eleven years old," he observed in a matter-of-fact manner. "I think now is a good time for you to start learning about the family business. You will go to work with me tomorrow." Now that I was twelve, I was already an experienced employee.

Papa had served in the military when he was younger. It was after leaving the military that he started his business. By the time I was born, he had already become a major distributor of bottled drinks, a variety of manufactured items, and fruits, vegetables, and coffee from several farms. He owned multiple trucks and operated three stores, two wholesale and one retail. Maman managed the retail store, which was the smallest of the three enterprises.

Papa never told my sisters to go to help my mother at her store during the summers, but because I was a boy, I had to be trained for work outside the home. Papa assumed that his daughters would one day marry and stay home to care for their own families. The irony that his own wife worked with him in business was apparently lost on him. I never asked Francoise or Marie-Jeanne how they felt about this arrangement, and they never volunteered an opinion. In retrospect, I think they were quite content to sleep in every morning.

I did not go to the store every day. On one or two days each week, I would wake to find that Papa had already left home and I was free to relax and play all day with my sisters and brothers. The truth is I did not really mind going to work. Waking up early was the hardest part. Once I got to the store, I quite enjoyed being there. At the smaller of the two wholesale establishments, Papa had taught me how to count money, take stock, and track sales. It was not long before he would leave me in charge of the store for brief periods of time. He would instruct me to supervise the employees in his absence, and when he returned, I had to report on what the workers and I had accomplished and provide an accounting of all sales and remaining inventory.

Sometimes the numbers did not add up, and my father would ask questions to help me figure out where the error had occurred. "Did you buy lunch for the men and for yourself again?" he would ask. Usually

I nodded yes. Papa knew I liked to play the role of the "boss man" and that I had a good relationship with the workers in the store. As I was the owner's son, they showed me a great deal of respect, and in return I often handed them money from the cash register to buy sodas and lunch. I would also help myself to a few coins so I could buy candy.

Occasionally one or two items from the store would be missing, and I would be unable to provide an explanation. It was always embarrassing to have to confess to Papa that I had no idea what had happened. On these occasions Papa would take the opportunity to remind me that operating a business was a serious undertaking and that I needed to remain vigilant. "You cannot assume everyone is trustworthy," he would say. "You will lose money and products if you are not diligent and attentive at work. Stay focused. This is business!"

Even though he occasionally reprimanded me, I knew Papa was proud that he could leave me to supervise his business at such a young age. It also helped that the workers liked me and considered it an honor that my father would trust them to look out for the well-being of his young son. Papa was also confident that the workers would follow whatever instructions I gave them on his behalf.

I might have taken this "boss man" role a bit too much to heart because I saw it as my right to give directions to the workers at home too. Perhaps my mother was seeking to temper this sense of superiority when she announced that I was now old enough to wash my own clothes. I wasn't pleased that she was asking me to do the work that Chantal had always done for our family, but I knew better than to argue with Maman. Instead, I bundled my clothes and went in search of Chantal. When I couldn't find her anywhere, I approached Christophe, thrust the clothes at him, and instructed him to wash them.

Not yet thirteen, I was already a head taller than Christophe, who was a full-grown man. But he was not about to be pushed around by the insufferable likes of me. "No," he said shortly. "Your mother told you to wash them." With that, he turned and walked away from me. Infuriated, I ran after him and delivered a swift kick to the side of his leg.

Whap! Christophe whirled on me, replying with a hard, open-palmed slap to my upper arm. I rocked backward, stunned. I glared at our cook, and he stared back at me with eyes narrowed and jaws clenched. Things had never gone this far before. Prior to this I had only expressed my disdain for the household staff verbally and only when my parents were not within earshot. I had never assaulted any of them before. And most definitely, prior to that afternoon, none among them had ever struck me.

We had employed various cooks and housekeepers over the years. Some worked in our home for years, others for only a few months. I now wonder whether I was partially responsible for the turnover. Perhaps not all of them; there were at least a couple whom Maman told to leave because she suspected them of stealing or because they had broken an item that she really valued while sweeping the floor or dusting the furniture.

I cannot blame my parents for the bad attitude I cultivated toward the people who worked in our home. Papa and Maman did not explicitly tell us to be respectful toward them, but neither did they set a bad example by treating these workers poorly. As I recall, they did not seem to engage with them very much at all. Christophe and Chantal knew exactly what to do, and they did it with little obvious direction from my parents. They were employed to serve us, and that is exactly what they did—dutifully and quietly. They must have looked forward to those times when we would go away for the holidays. Other than a couple of Sundays each month, those were the only times that they would go to their own homes to be with their families. Even on Sundays, one of them would always remain on duty to serve us while the other got the day off. Their lives revolved around meeting our personal needs and ensuring that our house and the entire compound were clean, neat, and protected.

I treated Victor, our watchman and gardener, differently than I did Christophe and Chantal. I viewed him as a friend. There were several reasons for that. Victor had the key to the gate, and he could keep a secret. He sometimes allowed me to go out of the compound to play with my friends when my parents were not at home. I also liked his cooking. I think some of the animosity between Christophe and me stemmed from the fact that I told everyone how much I preferred Victor's cooking. Victor's ugali, a dish he made from cornmeal and the vegetables in our garden, was delicious, and I would intentionally hang around his outdoor "kitchen" whenever he was cooking. My mother did not want me to eat with him, but when she wasn't at home, I would secretly disobey her wishes.

In contrast I would shout orders at Christophe and Chantal that I expected them to obey and would often threaten to tell my parents if I observed them commit even a minor infraction. So when Christophe slapped me, my immediate response was to say, "I will tell Maman as soon as she gets home! She will tell you to leave our house immediately!"

Christophe merely looked at me and went on his way. But I never did tell Maman about that incident. In the hour or two before she and Papa came home, I replayed in my mind what had happened and realized that Maman would ask Christophe why he had hit me. I could not predict how she would react when she learned I had kicked him first, and for no good reason. My mother was a gentle and polite woman, and she expected her children to behave similarly. I suspected she would be ashamed of me and perhaps even become angry. No, I decided, I would say nothing and trust that Christophe would do the same. Christophe continued to work with us after that incident, but we hardly ever spoke to each other again.

Although I asked God to forgive me for my attitude long ago, it still makes me cringe with shame that I once harbored such ugly feelings. I was certainly old enough to have known that kicking the cook was wrong. And the irony of it all was that it was the people whom I mistreated and looked down on as inferior that God would use to protect me when death and destruction were unleashed in Kigali and I was in a most vulnerable position. I have never forgotten that lesson. Through God's grace, it would forever change my attitude and my behavior toward the poor and the weak.

CHAPTER 3

Sowing the Seeds

There was nothing particularly remarkable about my childhood. From a distance of years, I think of it as wonderfully normal, serene, and uneventful. I went to school, worked with Papa sometimes, watched television, played with my siblings, and celebrated weddings, birthdays, and holidays with family and friends in their homes or in ours. Perhaps my favorite thing to do on a Saturday was to go with Maman to Nyamirambo Market. When our driver was available, my sisters would join us. If he happened to be busy running errands for Papa, Maman and I would take the bus. I especially enjoyed it when it was just the two of us. I looked forward to having my mother's undivided attention away from the rest of the family. The highlight of market day was eating lunch with her after we had completed all the shopping.

The market was clean and well organized, with clearly designated areas for clothes, shoes, fruits, vegetables, makeup and other cosmetics, electronics, and pretty much anything else one might want to eat, wear, or use in daily life. By the time we were ready to head home at the end of the day, Maman and I had usually accumulated more bags and boxes than we could carry. Several teenage boys would immediately rush over to us after we finished eating and ask to help carry our merchandise to the bus. Maman would point to the first two or three who asked, and together we all would head to the bus stop, arms full of food and personal items. After the boys had loaded our items onto the bus, Maman would put money into their outstretched palms, and we would settle down in our seats for the ride home.

Another group of boys would be waiting for us at the end of the bus ride. They would carry our bags and boxes up the steep hill to our compound, where we would be greeted by Victor and Christophe at the gate. The men would relieve the boys of their load as Maman reached into her purse to reward the boys for their hard work. Their wide eyes and beaming smiles indicated that Maman must have paid them more than they were used to receiving for such trips. As they ran off, they would turn and wave, shouting thank you multiple times until they rounded the bend in the road and were out of sight.

My parents were kind people. Although neither they nor I appreciated the significance of this fact at that time, I know without a doubt that their generosity protected me during the horror that was to come.

Strangely, I envied these boys who carried our heavy loads. Although they wore no shoes and their clothes were torn and dirty, they seemed carefree and happy. As Maman and I ate lunch at the market, I would observe them, hair uncombed and faces streaked with dirt and sweat, as they wandered through the aisles, playing and laughing together before rushing to offer help to a customer who had signaled the need for assistance. I would watch them wistfully as they sat together, counting and comparing their earnings before running off to buy sweets and other treats. Like me, several were not yet teenagers.

To my young eyes, they appeared to be cheerful and untroubled, with no adult telling them what to do.

On one occasion when my parents were not at home, I convinced Victor to allow me to leave the compound for an hour. Once outside our front gate, I took the bus to the market and attempted to imitate these boys by approaching shoppers and offering my assistance. I was completely unaware that my fine clothing and well-groomed appearance gave me away as a privileged outsider and that I looked completely out of place in the role I was trying to assume. I was doomed to fail.

"What is your name?" demanded the first woman I approached as she slowly looked me up and down for clues to my family ties. "Who is your father?" inquired another as she stared at the nice pair of shoes I was wearing. "You are not supposed to be doing this kind of work," one gentleman told me. Reaching into his pocket, he added, "Here is some money for bus fare. Take it and go home before you get into trouble." Suddenly it occurred to me that I might encounter a friend of my parents. What explanation would I give them for hustling for tips in the market? If they reported what I was doing, Papa would surely spank me, and he would definitely be ashamed. I hurriedly boarded the next bus home with not even a single coin to show for my entrepreneurial efforts.

On Sundays we went to church. It mattered very much to my mother that we attended as a family. Although we were officially Protestant, we went to St. Charles Lwanga Catholic Church almost as often as we went to St. Etienne Anglican Church. The Catholic church was a fifteen-minute walk from our compound, so when Papa was not available, we would walk there. When Papa was able to join us, we would all drive to St. Etienne, which was further away. My sisters and I took confirmation classes there in preparation for receiving Holy Communion. Both churches were impressive structures, with tall white walls and stained-glass windows on the outside and shiny gilded furnishings on the inside. The Anglican Church also had a distinctive green roof that caused it to stand out among the other buildings near the city center.

Sometimes my sisters and brothers would stay home when Papa was not going to church. But if Maman was going—and she did almost every Sunday—she would insist that I go with her. I am not sure why she singled me out to accompany her, but I am glad she did. Even as a child, I felt changed when I went to church. I can't describe my feelings exactly, but I definitely felt closer to God. Going to church inspired me to pray. I remember asking God to protect me from Papa's scolding and for forgiveness when I made a mistake. I was also focused and very interested in everything that the pastor, priest, or Sunday school teacher taught me. The Bible stories especially riveted me, and I eagerly anticipated hearing new ones each week. Being in church caused me to experience inexplicable joy. *This is where life is*, I thought. I sometimes wonder if Maman noticed the special effect that church had on me back then and that was why she always brought me with her. She noticed many things, even though she did not always say very much.

Christmas was a very exciting time at our house. Maman and Papa always bought the six of us new shoes and new clothes, and my siblings and I loved to show off our outfits at church on Christmas morning. We were not the only ones. The entire community would be in attendance, decked out in their new outfits, anxious to see and be seen. But church was more than just a social occasion for me. Even when I was young, the story of Jesus's birth and life resonated with me. So much so that I now believe that during my elementary school years, Jesus was at work in me even though I did not yet have a personal relationship with him. But like soil being tilled and fertilized in preparation for the farmer's seeds, going to church with my family during my childhood prepared my ears, mind, and heart to hear, believe, and love Jesus later on when I was given the choice to follow or ignore him.

While I listened closely to the lessons shared in church, I was not nearly as focused in school. It was now early in 1993, and I was thirteen years old. The results of the all-important national examination that was administered to students at the end of grade six had just been released, and I had not done well at all. Unlike my sisters, who excelled in their academic classes, I was an average student. My interests skewed more toward music and soccer with my classmates during the week and family outings and games with my siblings on the weekends. Homework and studying received minimal attention. Although I admitted it to no one at the time, my lack of interest in schoolwork was partly influenced by the fact that Papa had money. Why did I need to work hard in school if I would one day take over the management of his successful business?

My father was not of the same mindset, however. "What have we not given you, Bosco?" he asked me on the evening that he received my national exam results. "What have we not done for you?" Papa's voice was soft, and there was no anger in his eyes, just a weariness I had not noticed before. I was used to his angry reprimands, but this time was different. His low tone unnerved me. His obvious frustration made me sad. I had disappointed my Papa terribly.

My parents wanted my sisters and me to have the best education available in Rwanda, and they insisted we do our part by working hard. My elementary school was one of the best, attended by the children of many high-ranking residents of the city, including Rwanda's president. My sisters went to a different school that was equally prestigious, even though they insisted that because their school had a second floor, it was superior to mine, which was located in a single-story red brick building.

From my parents' perspective, my poor performance on the national examination had serious ramifications for my future. Only the students with the highest scores earned a seat in one of the tuition-free, highly selective, well-regarded government high schools, which started in grade seven. Those who scored below the required score could still enter grade seven at a good private high school if they passed that school's own examination *and* were able to pay the school fees. Those unable to attend a government or private high school for academic or financial reasons would have no option but to attend a trade school. Both of my older sisters had scored well enough on the national examination to secure spots in excellent government schools. I was secretly mortified by the idea that I might have to attend one of the low-rated trade schools.

"Starting today you will be responsible for your future." Papa's voice jolted me back into the present. "I have done all I can. Now it is up to you." What did he mean? Papa and Maman had always taken care of everything. I felt sorry for myself and wished I had studied harder for the exam. "Here is what you will do," Papa continued. "Go down to the Anglican church and inquire whether their high school, Petit Seminaire, has space for you. If you are lucky, you may be able to get in." With that, he turned and walked out of the house, got in his car, and was gone.

I got dressed and took the bus to the Anglican church. I felt nervous. My father had just told me that my future was in my own hands, and I was not sure if I could handle the responsibility. When I arrived at the church, a woman directed me to the administrator in charge of school admissions. I got to the point immediately.

"Good afternoon," I said. "I would like to attend Petit Seminaire. Is there space for me there?"

The gentleman was surprised by my abrupt delivery, and he looked around to see if there was someone else standing behind me. I could tell by his furrowed brow that he was surprised I had come by myself. With a shrug he responded, "Yes, there are a few spaces still available, but you will have to pass the entrance examination to qualify." He then wrote the date, time, and location of the examination on a sheet of paper and handed it to me. "Make sure you are not late," he said. I took the note, thanked him, and headed home.

With a new resolve, I studied and prayed in the days before the examination. I was determined to pass, and I had convinced myself that success was dependent on the intensity and fervor with which I did both. To my relief and Papa's joy, this strategy worked. I passed the test and was offered one of the last remaining spots at Petit Seminaire.

CHAPTER 4

Growing Unrest

Lake Muhazi is a thin, narrow body of water that extends into the town of Kibungo in the southeastern region of the country. Petit Seminaire is strategically located on a hill overlooking a portion of the lake's twenty-five square kilometers of surface area. I still remember the excitement I felt when I viewed the expanse of water for the first time through the open window of Papa's car. As we made the final ascent toward the school, I gazed into the picturesque valley below, and a smile curled my lips. *I will get to wake up to this amazing view every morning for the next six years,* I thought. I was feeling very pleased with myself. I had gained admission to Petit Seminaire, a well-respected private boarding school, which had made Papa very proud.

Deep in my thoughts for much of the journey, I had failed to take note of the exceptional beauty of the Rwandan countryside. Not until I returned to my homeland many years later did I truly appreciate the breathtaking scenery visible at every turn—the rich red earth, lush vegetation, rolling hills and towering mountains, and wide expanses of grassy fields. But the unexpected appearance of Lake Muhazi, shimmering below us in the late-morning sunshine, caused me to sit up and finally take in my surroundings near the end of our sixty-kilometer drive.

The excitement and fear that had gripped my stomach in recent days suddenly intensified as we drove through a large gate and my new boarding school came into full view. I had not admitted it to anyone, but I was afraid to leave home and all that was familiar. Papa was stern sometimes, but I knew he loved me, while Maman encouraged and indulged me. My brothers and sisters were my best friends, and I would miss them, even Claudine. On the other hand, going to secondary school meant I was no longer a child. I looked forward to the freedom of living on my own away from my parents' constant gaze and discipline. I was also comforted in knowing that I would see my family during the school holidays.

The night before Maman had come into my bedroom to squeeze a few last-minute items into my stuffed bags and to reassure herself that everything I needed for school was securely packed away. Then she sat on the edge of my bed and looked me in the eye. "My son, please listen to me," she said seriously. "Some of those girls in high school do not behave properly. Many have HIV and AIDS. If you don't do what is right, I will lose you." I was shocked. We had never spoken about male-female relationships before, and I was extremely embarrassed by her decision to counsel me in this manner on the eve of my departure. Before I could respond, however, she drew me close, put her hand on my head, and began to pray for me. Embarrassment was replaced by peace as she prayed. When she was finished, she gave me a warm hug.

I am sure my mother prayed for me on other occasions. However, that prayerful embrace the night before I left for boarding school is my most vivid memory and one that I will always treasure. Her embrace filled me with so many emotions—belonging, safety, confidence, strength, peace, love. Years later I would conclude that the Holy Spirit had filled my room that night, beckoned by my mother's fervent pleas on my behalf.

Now, as I stood outside the school office waiting for Papa to pay my school fees and get answers to the few remaining questions he had, I thought longingly of Maman and tried not to cry. I had received special permission to check in a few days early, so there weren't many students around. Thankfully no one witnessed my tears. Minutes earlier Papa had helped me carry my bags to my dormitory room, which included four bunk beds. I staked my claim to one of the bottom bunks by putting my bags on the mattress. "The top bed is hard to reach," I told Papa. "It will be easier to make up the one on the bottom."

Papa was very quiet as we walked toward his parked car. We stood beside the open car door in awkward silence. Then my father said firmly, "Study hard, Bosco. If you do not do your work, you will be on your own." He reached over and pulled me to his chest in a very quick embrace before releasing me and slipping behind the steering wheel. As he drove away, he turned his head and gave a quick wave. I could see that his eyes, like mine, glistened.

Although I did not know exactly what my father meant when he said I would be "on my own" if I did not do my work, I did not want to find out. So for perhaps the first time ever, I applied myself diligently to both classwork and homework. To my surprise and relief, I began to earn good grades. I also got along well with my classmates. Shortly after I had arrived, an older boy had told me that new students were relegated to the bottom bunks and were responsible for making up the beds of the older boys, who typically selected the upper bunks. Armed with this insider information, I had quickly moved my belongings to a top bunk. I was then able to convince my new, unsuspecting roommates, who arrived several days later, that I was entitled to the same deferential treatment that the boys on the other top bunks demanded. In this way, I deviously avoided responsibility for making my bed. The older boys thought I was rather clever for manipulating my peers in this way, and I enjoyed their admiration.

Petit Seminaire shared its large campus with a government high school called Grand Seminaire and a community hospital. Grand Seminaire was in a more modern and much larger two-story building, whereas the single-story building that housed Petit Seminaire was smaller. However, in all other respects, both schools were similar: academically rigorous, clean, and attractively landscaped. Students from each school attended classes in their respective buildings but shared dining and living spaces.

The green hills that surrounded the campus were dotted with small, thatch-roofed homes. The local residents were primarily farmers, although a few fishermen who relied on the lake for their income also lived nearby. The area was sparsely populated, with much of the land dedicated to growing bananas and peanuts. From our classrooms we would often observe our neighbors in the distance, sweeping their dirt yards or tending their crops. The most impressive structure in the vicinity was a large house that belonged to the local bishop, a well-known and highly respected man in the community, whom we rarely saw. There were also a few small shops within walking distance of the campus that sold soda, snacks, and food items. For anything else, I would board a bus and travel for fifteen minutes into town, where there was a market and several larger stores. Being able to go and come as I wished on the weekends gave me a feeling of independence.

One of my favorite weekend activities was to take the short walk from campus down to the lake. My classmates and I would play games on the grassy shore or sit on the dock and fish while dipping our feet in the crystal-clear water. Many of the boys would swim out to the deep, but not me. I could not swim and was content to splash around in the shallows. We would lie in the sun afterward talking about our lives back home, our families, our teachers, and any number of mundane topics. Some of the students would also wash their clothes at the lake. Even though there was a designated place to do laundry back at the school, swimming and fishing while one's clothes lay drying on the hot rocks next to the lake alleviated the drudgery of the task.

While there were no desperately poor students enrolled at my school, many of my peers came from families that were not as affluent as mine. After paying for school fees, these students' parents could not afford to provide their children with much pocket money. With little or no money of their own, these students could only stare longingly as the wealthier students headed to the shops and returned to campus with pockets full of savory snacks and sweets.

But my classmates were entrepreneurial problem-solvers. To address this disparity in resources, individual business arrangements were often negotiated between students who had pocket money and those who did not. I had never had to wash my own clothes at home, for example. Even after my mother directed me to take on this chore, I sneakily managed to get Chantal to keep doing it. My clumsy efforts to wash my clothes at school revealed to everyone that I needed help. Two of my classmates approached me with an offer to perform this task on a weekly basis in exchange for a share of my pocket money and free access to my laundry soap for their clothes as well. In less than a minute, we struck a deal. Arrangements like this were commonplace on campus. But I treated my helpers at school with the utmost respect, unlike the way I treated household staff back home. They were older and bigger, and I was keenly aware that I was at their mercy.

Everything was going well for me during the first trimester of the school year when I became sick with nausea and intense stomach pain and was sent home by the school administrators. The doctor in Kigali found nothing wrong with me and suggested that perhaps my body just needed to adjust to the different kinds of food served at school. My parents and siblings teased me that I was simply homesick. After a couple of days at home, I felt better and returned to school. But a few weeks later, just before dawn, the pain once again woke me out of a deep sleep. I could see the silhouettes of my roommates and hear them snoring in their beds as the waning moonlight peered through a small window in the corner. The spasms were more intense than before. I bit my lower lip to contain the moan. *Not again,* I thought. I tossed and turned, trying to find a position that would ease my discomfort. Before the end of the day, I was back in Papa's car, heading toward home.

This time my treatment and recuperation took longer. I was hospitalized briefly, and in addition to new medication, the doctor put me on a restricted diet. I was quite weak and stayed in bed or reclined in the living room for almost two weeks. Although I did not say anything to my parents, I was happy to be home for reasons that had nothing to do with all the pampering I was receiving from Maman and my sisters. It was around February of 1994, and I could no longer ignore the growing turmoil on campus. In truth, the underlying tension had been evident almost from the moment I arrived on campus, but I had pretended not to notice. Rather naively I had thought that things would get better. They did not. By early 1994 the situation was decidedly worse.

Students had begun to identify with the various political parties that were forming around the country. They often argued fiercely with each other in a vain attempt to sway opinions on issues I knew little about. I also noticed that after class ended each day, many of the older students formed groups that were increasingly drawn to the newspapers and radios. I wished they would play soccer instead because I did not like the effect that this preoccupation with the media was beginning to have on the student body. The news seemed to inflame some of them and stoke their anger. For other students, the radio announcements evoked deep concern, even fear. One popular radio station, called RTLM, played music that appealed to many of the students. However, its announcers also criticized the president for engaging in peace talks with Tutsi leaders and promoted "Hutu Power" while degrading Tutsis by referring to them as cockroaches who should be exterminated. Without a doubt the commentary that accompanied those broadcasts played a significant role in inciting conflicts at my school and eventually the violence that would overwhelm the country.

I dreaded the loud animated arguments that often followed these broadcasts. It took only one carelessly thrown fist for pandemonium to break loose in the school yard. On more than one occasion, small fights between handfuls of students had evolved into full-fledged campus riots. The boys in grades nine through twelve were becoming increasingly aggressive, and they scared me. Their anger was raw and intense, and I, along with many of my classmates in grade seven, did not want to be a part of it. We tried to become inconspicuous by quietly doing our work or reading in our rooms. Occasionally we would retreat to the lake or to town to get away from the disturbances.

My older peers had become obsessed with ethnic identity. Like so many others, I had a Hutu parent and a Tutsi parent, and my fourteen-year-old brain could not logically process how a person like me could possibly choose one ethnicity over the other. And why was it suddenly so important? My parents never discussed the topic, and I had only discovered the ethnic identities of my parents quite by accident.

Several years before, when I was in elementary school, a teacher had asked me if I was Hutu or Tutsi. I was puzzled by the question. She sent me home with instructions to return with an answer the following day. I remember Maman was reluctant to tell me. It was only after I explained that I might be punished for not obeying the teacher that she relented and, with a dismissive wave of her hand, said, "Just tell her you are Hutu."

But I pressed for more information. "Are you Hutu, Maman?"

Turning to go, she responded, "That's not important, Bosco."

I followed her into the kitchen. "But I want to know," I insisted.

"I am Tutsi," she finally said before adding, "but it doesn't matter. We are all Rwandan."

Now, only a few years later, I began to suspect that Maman was wrong. It mattered very much. "Do you remember when those men put Papa in prison?" I asked my sisters from my reclined position on the living room couch. My question startled Francoise and Marie-Jeanne, who had been quietly reading. I was going back to school the next day, and the three of us were enjoying each other's company in silence. I knew they were sad that I would be leaving. I wasn't happy to be going back to school either. Although my stomach no longer hurt and I had finished all the medicine the doctor had prescribed, I nevertheless had a very uneasy feeling.

At my question, my sisters looked up at me from their books. "How could we forget?" Francoise replied softly.

I was about ten or eleven years old on the evening when Maman came home crying and blurted out, "Papa will be gone for a while." We were used to Papa traveling for work, so we were perplexed that news of what we assumed was another business trip had brought Maman to tears. After Maman regained her composure, Claudine peppered her with questions, and eventually the detail Maman wanted to hide from us came out. "Your Papa is in jail, and I don't know when they will release him," she told us. She was trying so hard to be brave for us, but a lone tear rolled down her cheek.

We soon learned that Papa and several other businessmen had been accused of funding a political party that opposed the government and had been arrested. I didn't ask Maman whether the accusation was true, in part because I didn't really understand. No one at home or at school taught us about law, government, or politics, so I had no appreciation of the seriousness of the charge. I was also afraid that discussing the answer to that question with us children might distress Maman further. Her voice quivered, and pressing her palms to her cheeks, she rocked gently back and forth as she spoke to us. I knew instinctively that Maman was afraid that Papa would be killed.

Papa remained locked up for about two weeks. During that time several men whom we did not know came to search our house. We were terrified when they barged into our home unexpectedly one night after dinner. I don't know if they ever found what they were looking for, but I remember that Maman cried for a long time after they left.

Maman had tried to take Papa food in jail but had been turned away each time. When he finally came home, he looked terrible. He was so thin that I wondered if he had eaten anything at all while he was gone. Papa said nothing to us children about what had happened to him. I am not sure if he even spoke to Maman about his time in prison. Rwandan men often confide in their male friends rather than in their wives. That's just the way it is in our culture. I suspected that if anyone had been privy to the details of Papa's ordeal, it would have been one of his closest male friends. Because we never discussed it, life soon returned to normal. It was as if Papa had never been jailed.

"Why are you thinking about all that now, Bosco?" Marie-Jeanne interrupted my ruminations with her question. "It happened a long time ago."

I looked cautiously over my shoulder before responding. I didn't want Claudine or my brothers to hear what I was about to say. "I remember there was talk of arrests, killings, foreign invaders, and burnings of people's homes back then," I whispered. "And those same kinds of things are being reported on the radio and television now. In fact, now I think the situation might even be much worse."

Marie-Jeanne shrugged. "I don't know that it's any worse," she said. "I think it just seems that way because we are older. We know more about what's going on. Papa and Maman can't hide the news from us like they did before." Francoise nodded silently in agreement.

In at least one regard, Marie-Jeanne was right. Back in the early 1990s, Papa and Maman had shielded us from political news and reports that discussed conflicts between Hutus and Tutsis. Now that we were older, it was almost impossible for Papa and Maman to control our access to the radio and newspaper. And they certainly could not keep our schoolmates from talking. Hostility and fear were growing in the country. Even we children could sense it. Yet Papa and Maman still refused to discuss any of it at home, so my sisters and I did not fully grasp the danger that was spreading in the early months of 1994.

The next day I returned to school on the bus. Papa had decided that I was capable of traveling alone between home and school when I was well. I didn't mind at all. Traveling alone made me feel all grown up. Fortunately, I was able to complete the remainder of the second trimester of grade seven without any more medical emergencies. I had missed almost ten days of school because of my illness, so I fully immersed myself in my studies. Working hard served two purposes:

my grades steadily improved as I caught up on missed assignments, and studying served as a welcome diversion from the negativity that permeated the airwaves and conversations on campus.

Most of my teachers avoided any mention of the growing political tensions and focused exclusively on the curriculum. My history teacher, who also taught us hygiene, continued to emphasize the importance of washing our hands and cutting our fingernails. Even in the waning days of the trimester, as reports came in from around the country of people being killed or chased from their burning homes, our teacher continued to extol the virtues of manicured fingernails. I confess that at the time, I appreciated her focus on the trivial. It helped to reassure me that despite what the older boys were saying, conditions were not as bad as they seemed.

My music teacher was another source of distraction. He was from Burundi, and his strong accent coupled with the strange way he pronounced certain words triggered our laughter whenever his back was turned toward us. It is very likely he knew that my classmates and I secretly made fun of him. That would explain the harsh manner in which he spoke to us and the excruciating assignments he doled out, such as requiring that we sing and write the musical notes for entire songs within unreasonably short periods of time.

Finally the trimester came to an end. Excitedly I packed my bags to head home for the Easter holiday. The past month had been difficult for so many reasons, and I looked forward to a relaxing two-week break at home with my family before the third and final trimester of grade seven began. As I waved goodbye to my classmates on that last day at school, I had no way of knowing that I would never again enjoy the waters of beautiful Lake Muhazi with them or that some who smiled and waved back at me would be dead in less than one month.

PART TWO

Things Fall Apart

CHAPTER 5
Death on the Doorstep

"They came in out of nowhere!" My sister Francoise paced back and forth across my bedroom floor, clenching and unclenching her fingers. Her bottom lip trembled as she continued. "The men just pushed open the door and came in. They told us to be quiet or they would kill us. They had guns, Bosco. They pointed guns at us!"

I had arrived at the entrance to our compound only minutes before, a suitcase in each hand. I was in a good mood as I greeted Victor, our watchman and gardener, with a friendly grin when he opened the gate to my knock. But before we were able to exchange salutations, Francoise came running down the driveway. It was obvious that she had been waiting for me. She flung her arms around my neck and squeezed more tightly than usual as she planted a kiss on my cheek. "There is so much to tell you, Bosco," she said as she grabbed the suitcase in my left hand and hurried toward the house. "Come, let's go inside."

Something was wrong. I saw it in the way Victor peered nervously over my shoulder when he opened the gate for me as if he was expecting to see someone or something else behind me. Come to think of it, the street in front of our house had been eerily quiet. I had passed only one or two other pedestrians as I walked the last few meters home from the bus stop. The streets should have been busier at this time of the day. A cloud of foreboding settled over me. Francoise was always happy to see me, but she had never run to hug me like that before.

The moment I entered my bedroom, I saw the broken window. Shards of glass were scattered across the floor. I dropped my suitcase and slowly sat on the edge of my bed. I looked at my oldest sister for an explanation. Her words poured out as she paced back and forth between the door and the broken window.

The night before someone had hurled an incendiary device into our compound. It had landed on the grass outside of my bedroom, and the force of the explosion had shattered the window above my bed. The situation quickly deteriorated. Armed gunmen stormed into our compound after threatening to climb the wall and kill Victor if he did not open the gate for them. Within seconds, Francoise said, the men were standing in our living room, guns pointed at my sisters, brothers, and parents. I could not believe what I was hearing.

"Two of the men went into Papa's drawer in his bedroom, and they found a gun," my sister continued.

"They took it," Claudine chimed in. "Did you know Papa had a gun?"

Francoise and I spun around to find Marie-Jeanne and Claudine standing in the doorway. They had obviously been listening quietly for a while. Claudine had interrupted Francoise, her voice low and urgent as she told me about Papa's gun.

"No, Claudine," I responded. "I didn't know Papa had a gun." Turning back to Francoise, I asked the question that was now uppermost in my mind. "Where are Papa and Maman?"

Marie-Jeanne glanced at the clock on my desk. "They are working but will be home soon. They don't stay out after dark anymore."

Marie-Jeanne's brief explanation did little to comfort me. Things were changing, and I didn't understand why. I looked at my three sisters, hoping for more details. Their trauma was palpable. But despite their distress, I wanted to hear about everything that had happened. I did not want them to hold anything back. "They didn't hurt any of us," offered Francoise. She had seen the silent question in my eyes. I felt a rush of relief. My sisters had not been raped. Maman and Papa had not been shot. The situation was not as bad as it could have been.

Yet even as the mood of the country had worsened in recent months, my parents had still refused to discuss the national unrest with my siblings and me. All of us were aware that political turmoil had given rise to anger and anxiety around the country—the daily radio broadcasts were a constant reminder. But my parents continued to operate as if politics was a taboo subject. Perhaps because my father was Hutu and my mother was Tutsi, they resisted discussing these matters, both of them reluctant to criticize Hutus or Tutsis or the government. Or maybe they felt it would have been dangerous to engage in such conversations, even within the privacy of their home. It's also possible they simply wanted to preserve our innocence. There would be time enough for us to learn of these things, and they may have decided that there was no need to hasten the inevitable. By early 1994, however, I had begun to learn about current political developments on my own, haphazardly, from my peers at school. But I remained perplexed. *Why the hatred?* I wondered.

My parents were elated to see me when they arrived home that evening. As Francoise had done earlier, Maman gave me an especially tight hug. She and Papa asked me many questions about school over dinner, but they said nothing about the explosion, the broken window, or the home invasion by armed men. I took my cue from them and said nothing about these matters either. But as hard as they tried to create an air of normalcy, I would occasionally catch a faraway expression in Papa's eyes that revealed his burdened thoughts. Similarly, Maman's tense smile failed to hide her apprehension. Their faces were open books that communicated the truth they so desperately sought to hide from us children—they were afraid.

Later that evening Maman pulled me aside and said in as casual a tone as she could muster, "Sleep in the guest room tonight. Victor will fix your bedroom window in the morning." I peered into her eyes, seeking an assurance she was incapable of providing. Her eyes filled with tears. "Don't worry; everything will be all right," she whispered without conviction. My mother was a comforter by nature, but now she struggled to fulfill that role.

In the days leading up to Easter, we stayed close to home. My parents went to work in the mornings but did not venture out come evening. We didn't visit family or friends, which was unusual around the holiday season. No one came to visit us either. When we did go out to shop, we noticed that people no longer conversed freely. Most hurriedly concluded their business then retreated to their homes. There were more and more news reports of demonstrations happening around the country. By any measure, the situation was not normal.

I was disappointed but not entirely surprised when Papa announced on Easter morning that we would not be going to church. More than anything I yearned for the peace and quiet joy I always experienced within the walls of the sanctuary. Papa offered no explanation for his decision. None was necessary. We were all nervous and on edge, waiting for something to happen that would hopefully relieve the tension that permeated the city. My chest felt tight, as if I needed to exhale but was waiting for permission to do so and no one would grant it. So I kept holding my breath.

The Wednesday night following Easter Sunday, I lay in bed reading, oblivious that a plane carrying President Habyarimana and several of his associates was preparing to land at Kigali's international airport. He was returning from Tanzania, where he had attended a meeting with several other African leaders. Shortly after 8:00 p.m., missiles sliced the night sky over the city. At least one pierced the plane carrying President Habyarimana as it prepared to land. Everyone on board the aircraft was killed in the explosion. In an instant the tension that had been building for weeks, months, even years broke with a violent force. Not a single Rwandan living in the country would remain unscathed in the aftermath of that horrific release.

When I opened my eyes on the morning of Thursday, April 7, 1994, I awoke to a new world. The entire trajectory of my life had been altered by events that had occurred while I slept. Yet I remained woefully ignorant. I had shopping on my mind. Maman had promised that today she would take me to the market to buy some new shoes, pants, and a few shirts. I also needed notebooks and pens for school, which was scheduled to resume the following week. I was looking forward to our shopping trip, not only because I liked getting new clothes but also because going to the market with Maman was routine, something we had done for years, a familiar activity that would signal life returning to normal.

Then I heard them. Gunshots in rapid succession. It was not the first time since returning home that I had heard shooting in the distance, but usually it happened late at night, short intermittent bursts separated by a minute or two of silence. This morning, however, the gunshots were louder and more prolonged—and closer to our compound than before. The tightness in my chest returned.

I walked into the living room and saw Maman sitting by herself on the sofa, her ear pressed close to the radio. "Maman, are we going...."

She looked up and put her index finger to her lips to silence me. "We will not be going anywhere today," she said. "Go back to your room and turn on your radio. Listen, then come back and tell me what you hear."

I did as I had been told. The only sound that came from my radio was music. Slow, mournful music. *Almost like funeral music,* I thought. *But why?* After waiting for about fifteen minutes for a news report that never came, I returned to the living room. By then my sisters and brothers had joined Maman. They looked very downcast, and I realized then that something terrible had happened.

"What's going on?" I demanded. "Why is no one talking on the radio?"

As if on cue, a voice suddenly interrupted the musical interlude. In a very somber tone, the radio announcer told us to "be calm" and to remain indoors until further notice. The music resumed playing, and I turned to Maman.

"The president has been killed, Bosco," she said softly.

My eyes widened and my knees buckled as I sank into the nearest chair. *Maman must be mistaken,* I thought. From my childlike perspective, certain people were beyond the reach of death. People like the president were too important, too powerful, to be subject to death. He was the leader of my country, a permanent fixture. How could he be dead? But he was dead. He and his traveling companions had been blown out of the sky in an instant.

A moment later loud gunshots, screaming, and shouting from just beyond the wall of our compound abruptly pierced my consciousness. Papa rushed into the living room. "Quick, everyone, go into your bedrooms." He paused. Then, in a whisper he added, "Lie quietly under your beds."

As my sisters and I rushed to our respective rooms, I noticed that Maman and Papa took my younger brothers, then eleven and nine years old, with them into their room. Pausing briefly in front of my parents' bedroom door, I saw Papa gently push Niyitegeka under the bed next to Maman and Twahirwa, who were already positioned to receive him. From his crouched position, Papa glanced up at me. Our eyes locked briefly before he motioned with his head for me to run along. Seconds later I, too, was under my bed.

Sporadic gunfire continued throughout the day. Everyone, including my cousin Thomas; our business manager, Francois; and our household staff, Christophe and Chantal, stayed under our beds for most of the day. We emerged only briefly to eat and to get updates from Victor, who remained outside in his shelter by the front gate. Periodically he would open the gate just a crack to see what was happening in the street and a few minutes later would meet with Papa at the front door to report on what he had seen. I noticed that he trembled and shook his head repeatedly as he spoke, as if trying to dislodge the vision of what he had witnessed. Listening to him, Papa would cover his face and then his mouth with his hands. Their physical distress conveyed more powerfully than words ever could the horror of what was unfolding outside.

"Victor said that there are a lot of men and boys with guns and machetes running up and down the street," Papa said when he came back into the living room. "They have entered some of the compounds nearby and have told the people who live there to come outside." Papa hesitated. It was obvious he did not want to tell us what had happened next. Looking at my youngest brother, he continued. "They have taken some of our neighbors away." Papa's attempt to shield us from the truth of our neighbors' fate did not fool anyone. Maman and my sisters started to cry. We all knew that our neighbors had been killed. We had heard the screams and the gunfire.

Early the next morning, Papa gathered us all together. "I do not think it is a good idea to hide under the beds anymore," he said. "I think it will be safer for us to hide in the ceiling." Leading us down the hallway toward the back of the house, he pointed above us. "There is a large gap between the ceiling and the roof right over here. No one will be able to find us if we crawl into that space." I do not know what my sisters thought about that idea, but for me, Papa's words created a feeling of desperation rather than confidence. I had never been so afraid in my life.

Two or three days later, the gang of armed men finally made their way to our compound. They had a name—the Interahamwe, which means "those who work together" or "those who fight together" in Kinyarwanda, Rwanda's national language. Later I would learn that *work* was being used as slang in anti-Tutsi radio broadcasts to mean *kill*. The Interahamwe were a government-supported militia that roamed the streets killing and terrorizing Tutsis, as well as any Hutus who dared to oppose or criticize them. Many of the Interahamwe were impoverished Hutu teenagers and young adults who had been easily recruited to the task with offers of money, drugs, alcohol, and guns, as well as the kind of power they would otherwise never have possessed. They wielded their newly acquired authority enthusiastically. Through Victor, we had learned that the Interahamwe were responsible for killing many of our neighbors and for mounting roadblocks throughout the city in an effort to find and execute as many Tutsis as possible.

The Interahamwe entered our home very suddenly. It happened

so quickly that we did not have time to climb up into the ceiling. Not that it would have done us much good. They had been monitoring the area for days and knew that no one had left our compound. We were cornered. Victor let the small mob through the gate. He had no choice, just as Papa was forced to open the front door under the threat of being shot. The rest of us hid in our rooms. We could hear the voices coming from the living room. The members of the Interahamwe told my father that they wanted money. A few minutes later, it became clear that the amount he had given them was not enough. "Where is your wife?" one of the men demanded. "Bring her to us right now."

I held my breath as I heard Maman walk out of her bedroom with Papa. Then I heard a voice issue a threat that almost caused my heart to stop beating. "Bring us more money now, or we will kill your Tutsi wife right here in front of you!" Papa must have complied almost immediately because I soon heard laughter and sounds of approval from the men. Shortly afterward they opened the front door and began to leave. A different voice shouted another warning as he walked down the driveway toward the front gate: "We will leave her today, but next time we will come back and kill her!"

Later that night Victor reported to my father that the men who had stolen our money had gotten into an argument over how to divide the cash among themselves. Victor was watching through a crack in the gate as they began to shoot at each other. Several were killed in the street, not far from our house. I secretly hoped that the man who had issued that final threat against my mother was among the dead.

When the Interahamwe returned a couple of days later, we once again hid in our rooms and braced for the worst. Papa later told us that although the group leader was the same, most of the men in the second group were different from the ones who had come before. In response to the new mob's demands, my father gave them all the remaining cash he had in the house, but it was not enough. "We know you," said one of the men. "You are a good man, but we will kill you if you do not have more money for us when we come again." After ransacking the kitchen and taking all the food they could carry, the men left us. Thankfully they did not ask for my mother.

In the years since, I have often replayed these two incidents in my mind. Why was my mother, a Tutsi, not killed when so many others like her had been slain nearby? One possibility was that my father was a well-known and respected Hutu businessman and had the cash that those men desperately wanted. Papa may also have told them my mother was Hutu. After marrying my mother, he may have secured a Hutu identity card for her, as some Hutu men married to Tutsi women were known to have done. Perhaps she showed the Interahamwe that card. But even if that was the case, Maman was tall and had the thin facial features associated with Tutsis. I doubt they would have believed she was Hutu.

Later I would learn that some of the young men who had descended on our compound were among those who had often carried Maman's bags from the bus stop after a day of shopping. They may have recalled her extreme generosity, and that, too, may have weighed in her favor. But none of those possibilities, alone or even together, can adequately explain why, on both days, our family was spared the horror that so many of our neighbors had endured during that murderous time. Even Hutus who were simply suspected of being sympathetic toward Tutsis were being massacred.

Looking back at these events through the lens of faith that I embraced years later, I now believe that the reason I did not witness my mother's murder was simple. Jesus intervened. And though I cannot explain the mystery of why he intervened on my behalf and not for so many others, it would definitely not be the last time.

CHAPTER 6
No Way Out

O vernight my father hatched an escape plan. Our situation was dire. Our food supply had been significantly depleted by the Interahamwe, who were continuing to kill people in their homes and on the streets. The money that had protected us so far was also gone. To remain in the house would mean certain death for Maman and possibly for the rest of us as well.

Early the next morning, Papa gathered us around to explain. "I will take the car and go to find some place safe for all of us to stay until this madness ends," he said. "If the Interahamwe ask where I am going, I will tell them I am going to get more money for them. I don't believe they will stop me. When I find somewhere safe, I will send a driver to get the rest of you."

The fight for control of Kigali had escalated in recent days. On one side were the Rwandan Army and their Interahamwe allies, and on the other were the forces of the Rwandan Patriotic Front (RPF), who were trying to stop the genocide that was underway. Comprised primarily of Tutsis, many of whom had been born outside of Rwanda to parents who had fled the country years earlier, the RPF had organized themselves into a military force that was now determined to defeat those who were bent on killing every Tutsi.

As a result of the intense fighting in and around the capital, the government-controlled radio station had started to encourage women and children to abandon the city before it "burned to the ground." However, men and boys older than twelve years were required to stay to "defend the city" against the RPF. Papa reasoned that it would be easier for us to leave after him with the wave of other women and children who had decided to heed the government's advice. I didn't want our family to be separated, but I had to agree with Papa. If we all left together, the men who wanted my father's money would know that my father had no intention of returning. We had to be strategic in our escape.

"Bosco, I need you to remain and help your mother and sisters," Papa told me now. "You are not very tall. Even though you are fourteen, the soldiers will not think you are big enough to hold a gun, much less fight." Papa tried to give me a reassuring smile. I nodded. I was relieved that he had asked me to stay with Maman. "I will take Twahirwa and Niyitegeka with me now," Papa continued. "They are too young to be expected to fight."

Papa and my brothers left almost immediately. They did not pack anything. Luggage would have revealed that they did not intend to return any time soon. We exchanged quick hugs at the front door, and with only the clothes on their backs and a few food items hidden in the glove compartment of the vehicle, they drove off. I stood at the window and waved until I could see them no more.

Shortly after noon the following day, a man I recognized as one of my father's employees arrived at our compound in Papa's car. He told us that Papa had instructed him to drive us to Gitamara, a town about forty kilometers away. Papa and my brothers had arrived there safely, he assured us, and Papa had rented a place where we could all stay. We were all so excited! Eager to be reunited in a safer location, we spent the afternoon packing the trunk of the car with clothes, food, a few personal items, and important documents that Maman decided we would need. That night I could hardly sleep.

I awoke early the following morning. The sun had not yet come up when I started to get dressed. After a quick breakfast, we locked up the house as securely as possible. "To prevent looting," Maman explained. I remember being puzzled by that. We were leaving the servants behind. The armed men could return and force them to open every room in the house. But I said nothing. If it made Maman feel better to lock up the house, then I would not upset her by pointing out the obvious.

The driver, Maman, and Claudine sat in the front seat of the car, while my older sisters and I climbed into the back. Maman had insisted that I wear shorts and that I slide down low in the seat, between my sisters. "Try to make yourself as small as possible next to your sisters," she urged me. In Rwanda only schoolboys in the elementary grades typically wore shorts, and Maman hoped they would therefore make me appear younger than my age.

We said goodbye to Chantal, Christophe, Francois, and Thomas and slowly drove down the driveway. "We will be back as soon as it's safe," said Maman to no one in particular. As we exited the compound, I turned around to wave to Victor. He waved back before closing the gate behind us. I knew that the Interahamwe were unlikely to harass Papa's employees since they would not be expected to have any money. Furthermore, they were all Hutu. Yet I was concerned for their safety, especially that of Victor and Francois, for whom I had special affection.

The first roadblock was less than a kilometer from our compound. As we drove toward it, we were relieved to see no evidence of the killings that had taken place in recent days. Mercifully, someone had removed the dead bodies and had spared us additional trauma. Only a few armed men, who glanced suspiciously at our vehicle, strolled through the streets.

We came to a stop in front of a makeshift barrier of tree branches, rocks, old mattresses, and rusty oil drums that blocked the roadway. A young man only a couple of years older than me slowly approached our vehicle, his large gun pointed toward the ground. "You are leaving us here all alone?" he asked us. He then pushed half his body through the open window on the driver's side of the vehicle and looked closely at each of us. Suddenly there was a spark of recognition in his eyes. He was one of the young men who had carried Maman's bags on multiple occasions from the bus stop to our compound. Maman recognized him as well and smiled. "We will be back," she assured him. "We are just going down the road to Gitamara. Not too far."

Three or four other men left their positions at the roadblock and gathered around our car. I recognized a couple of them as well. "Open the trunk," someone yelled behind us. Our driver complied. "We are here protecting you, so the least you can do is give us some of the food you have back here," one of the men said as he rummaged through our belongings. After taking almost half of our food, the men demanded cash from my mother. Satisfied with the amount she handed over, they removed the debris that blocked the road and waved us through. We drove on in silence.

A few minutes later, we arrived at the next roadblock. As our car coasted to a stop, I scanned the faces of the ten or so soldiers and Interahamwe who were standing guard. I recognized none of them. We were about three kilometers from home, so it was not surprising that these men were unfamiliar. One of the soldiers approached our vehicle, and after giving my mother and sisters a cursory glance, he stared directly at me. His eyes fixed on my face, he slowly and deliberately uttered words that caused my heart to sink: "Get out."

A gasp escaped Maman's lips. I climbed over Francoise to exit the vehicle. I did not want her to step out of the car and be even more exposed to the men who had gathered around. Looking skeptically at my shorts, the soldier asked me, "How old are you?" I thought about lying, but there was something in the soldier's eyes that told me he already knew. "I am fourteen," I whispered while trying to avoid his piercing gaze. The soldier motioned toward the trunk. "Get your things," he ordered. "You are not going anywhere. You must stay and fight the RPF with us." Then, turning to the rest of the family, he yelled, "Everybody get out of the car, and show us your identification cards."

Our driver was Hutu, and I was sure he would have had proof of it; otherwise, my father would not have sent him for us. It was clear he was the employee of a wealthy individual who had hired him to transport women and children out of the war zone. Even though he was an adult Hutu man who might otherwise be required to stay and fight, under the circumstances the soldier allowed him to proceed. My sisters and I presented the soldier with our school identification cards, which revealed nothing about our tribal identity. Our physical features were fairly ambiguous—we were a mix of Maman and Papa—but fortunately for us, the soldier presumed that we were all Hutu. Our mother was Tutsi, however, and she looked it. I felt like crying. Ever since leaving our compound, I had feared someone would ask Maman for her tribal identity card. Since I had never seen it, I did not know if it identified her as Tutsi or Hutu. But even if it said *Hutu* there was a real possibility that the Interahamwe would not believe it. The men who were milling around had already begun to hurl insults at my mother.

Tears filled her eyes as she dutifully offered her tribal identity card for the soldier to examine. I held my breath and grasped Francoise's hand.

The fact that she was not shot on the spot assured me that her card stated that she was Hutu; however, the angry stares and vicious insults directed toward her suggested that the Interahamwe may have thought her card was a forgery. Several had pointed their rifles at Maman as the soldier inspected her identity card. At last the soldier returned Maman's card, and she hastily put it away in her pocket. The Interahamwe lowered their guns as the soldier obviously in charge barked another order. "All of you get back in the car." He looked at me and added, "Except you."

Oblivious to the fact that she was still in mortal danger, Maman rushed toward me. She pleaded with the soldier to change his mind. As she begged him to let me go, she whispered in my ear, "Don't worry; Papa will come back for you."

The soldier was resolute. Ignoring Maman, he continued to speak directly to me. "Walk back to your house now," he commanded. There was disdain in his voice, as if he thought I was a coward for trying to leave with women and children when there was a war to be fought. "Go! And if you turn to look back, we will shoot you on the spot."

My mother and sisters looked on in stunned silence as we all realized just how serious the situation had become. I extricated myself from Maman's arms and quickly walked to the trunk of the car to get my bag. A couple of the young men left their posts at the roadblock and followed me to see what else was in the trunk. They immediately helped themselves to all of our sugar and a significant quantity of our remaining food. As the two young men returned to their posts with our food, one of them apparently felt the need to explain his actions. "We are hungry," he said. "It's not right that we starve while we are protecting you."

I hoisted my bag over my shoulder and looked at Maman, Francoise, Marie-Jeanne, and Claudine. Tears streamed down their faces. "I'll be OK," I promised as I tried in vain to give them a reassuring smile. "See you soon." With a final quick wave, I turned around and started walking down the street in the direction of my home. With the soldier's warning ringing in my ears, I forced myself to keep my eyes straight ahead, even as Maman wailed and my sisters sobbed loudly behind me. I heard our driver plead with Maman to return to the vehicle. A few seconds later, I heard the car doors slam. I slowed my pace. I wanted to be sure my family was safely on their way before I moved out of earshot. As soon as I heard the car start and pull away, I exhaled. My family members had all made it through the roadblock and were safely on their way to Gitamara. I was simultaneously relieved and exceedingly distraught.

I felt numb. It was as if my limbs were moving on their own accord with little or no direction from my brain. As I made my robotic way back home, I was hardly aware of the people I passed along the way. They might as well have been trees. No one spoke to me, and I did not acknowledge anyone, not even with my eyes. My entire family was gone, and I was alone. Papa's plan had seemed so perfect. This was not supposed to have happened.

About thirty minutes later, the wall around our compound came into view. In response to my knock, Victor opened the gate slightly and peered through the crack. Seeing me, he immediately swung the gate wide open. "What are you doing here, Bosco?" he exclaimed. "Where is everybody?" He glanced up and down the street. "Why did you come back?"

Wearily, I walked toward the garage and took a seat in Victor's old wooden chair, which was positioned in front of the open door.

Thomas, Francois, Chantal, and Christophe came running out, alerted by Victor's shouts to my unexpected return. Their eyes grew wide as I described how Maman had made it past the Interahamwe at the second roadblock. Even Christophe, with whom I continued to have a strained relationship, expressed sympathy for me when he heard how I had been forced to walk away from my family under threat of being shot. After I finished talking, an uneasy silence enveloped us. No one seemed to know what to do or say in light of this troubling development.

Francois finally interrupted the silence. "Come, Bosco! Let's get something to drink. You must be thirsty after your walk." Without a word I followed him into the kitchen. Before being employed in my father's business, Francois had worked as a nanny and housekeeper in our home, starting long before I was born. Seeing his potential, Papa had paid for Francois's driving lessons and after a couple of years, promoted him to driver. In addition to driving Papa, Francois also took my mother and us children wherever we needed to go if Papa was not available. Eventually Papa promoted Francois again, this time to a management position in his business. Francois had continued to gain Papa's trust over the years and had become one of my father's closest confidantes. He was one of the few people who had copies of all the keys to the business. Everyone understood that he was Papa's second-in-command and a faithful and trustworthy manager, which put him unofficially in charge of the staff who remained at the compound.

Over the years Francois and I had developed a close relationship. Not only had he taught me how to ride a bicycle, but he had also risked Papa's wrath by secretly teaching me to drive the family car when I was only eleven years old. The depth of Francois's devotion, loyalty, and affection toward my family and me was unquestioned, and I was greatly relieved that in the absence of my parents, I could turn to him.

That night I chose to remain outside in the garage. For the first time ever, my home felt empty and unwelcoming. I did not want to sleep inside alone. Actually, I did not feel like sleeping at all. My body was tense, and my mind raced as I pondered questions for which I had no answers. Sitting with Victor and Francois in the dark was far preferable to the silence inside the house, where Maman's scent still lingered. We spent most of the night in quiet conversation that was interrupted sporadically by the rumble of explosions and bursts of gunfire in the distance. The battle for Kigali was underway, and we had no idea who was winning.

I must have dozed off eventually because I awoke to the smell of Victor's cooking. At his insistence I forced myself to eat a few mouthfuls of ugali before I turned to Francois and asked, "What is going to happen to me?" My father's manager flashed a reassuring smile and stated confidently, "Don't worry, Bosco. I know your father. Right this minute he is making plans for someone to come for you. I am sure of it. You will be all right."

Later that morning Francois, Victor, and I went for a short walk through the neighborhood. Initially, I had vehemently resisted the idea of leaving the compound. "It's much too dangerous," I insisted.

But Victor provided a very convincing, if disturbing, rationale for venturing out. "If we remain locked behind the gate, those men with the machetes and guns out there will think we do not approve of what they are doing," he argued. "They might kill us for being traitors." Francois nodded in agreement. "We must pretend," Victor continued. "If we go out briefly once or twice each day to greet them and offer them food, they will think we support them, and they will leave us alone."

And so, as difficult as it was for us to walk among those killers and greet them with a wave and a smile, that is exactly what we did.

To my dismay, a couple of them who recognized me from my trips to the market with Maman invited me to join them on their murderous hunt for Tutsis. One even went so far as to thrust a large gun into my hand. Before I could respond, Francois quickly intervened to diffuse the situation. "Look!" he said, pointing to my arms. "This boy is too skinny and weak to aim a gun properly. If he tries to shoot, he will probably drop the weapon and end up killing you and himself instead." The boys laughed as Francois took the weapon and returned it to the young man who had handed it to me. "Maybe next time," Francois said with a laugh before we continued strolling down the road.

As we headed back toward home, I felt nauseous. I barely noticed the vandalized and looted shops that we walked by or the mattresses and garbage strewn across every street. The only thing that penetrated my consciousness was that everyone we passed had a gun or a machete and the killers might return tomorrow and insist that I pick up arms and join them.

CHAPTER 7
Enemies All Around

The man standing before me was an imposing figure. He was not tall, but his military uniform strained to contain his thick arms and muscular shoulders. Moments earlier Victor had opened the gate to allow his car to enter the compound. As he stepped out of the vehicle, I approached him cautiously. My apprehension turned to joy when he informed me that Papa had sent him to get me. He explained that my family was safely settled in Gitamara and was eagerly awaiting my arrival. I could barely contain my excitement.

About three days had passed since the fateful day at the roadblock, where I had been forced to wave goodbye to my sisters and Maman. I had been sick with worry, wondering if they had made it to Gitamara. Victor and Francois had been very attentive to my needs, but it was not the same as being with my family. There was a dull ache in my chest that no amount of coddling and good food could relieve.

"Your father sent this money for you," the military officer said as he pulled out some folded bills from his wallet. "I will give you half of it now and give you the rest later when I return for you. I am a little short on cash at the moment. You understand, don't you?" He smiled as he asked me the question, but the smile did not reach his eyes. I nodded as I reached for the money in his outstretched hand. I was a boy, and he was a military officer. We both knew I was powerless to object. In any case, if that was the price for getting to my parents and siblings, then I was happy to let him take my money. In fact, I would gladly have given him all of it. Satisfied with my response, he continued, "I am busy right now, but I will return for you soon. Make sure you are ready to go when I return." With that, he turned and strode toward his car. I watched as he and his driver reversed out of the driveway, and with a quick wave, he was gone just as suddenly as he had appeared.

I ran into my bedroom to grab the bag that I had returned home with days earlier. It had sat undisturbed exactly where I had thrown it in the middle of my bed, unopened since my return. Having decided to stay outside with Victor in the garage rather than sleep in my own bed, I had gone into the house only to shower and change clothes. With toiletries and plenty of clothes still in my closet and drawers, there had been no reason to use the items in my small bag.

The military officer had given me no indication of when he might come back for me, but I wanted to be ready at a moment's notice. I carefully placed my bag beside the chair that served as my bed. For the remainder of the day, I paced up and down the driveway, too excited to sit or to eat, pausing to listen every time I thought I heard a car approaching our gate. That night was perhaps the longest of my life. I refused to believe the military officer would not return for me, but I was crushed with disappointment when it grew dark and still there was no sign of him.

My long wait ended the next morning when the officer, his driver, and another younger man in uniform, whom I presumed to be a fellow officer, came to pick me up. After a quick goodbye to Francois and the others, I climbed into the back seat next to the older officer, while the younger officer sat up front with the driver. The driver, whose name was Jacques, accelerated quickly through the streets of my neighborhood, slowing down only briefly at each roadblock to salute and be saluted by the men who were on guard. It was clear that my traveling companions were important men. No one told us to stop in order to display our identification.

As we neared the outskirts of Gitamara, the silence was suddenly destroyed by a spectacular burst of sounds—the ra-ta-tat of automatic rifle fire, exploding grenades, shouting, and the screeching of brakes. We were under attack by unseen assailants hiding in the hills that overlooked the road into Gitamara. They seemed intent on killing us! But for the skillful maneuvering of our driver, they would have succeeded. I looked out the window of our vehicle, mesmerized for several seconds by the sight of stones and dirt flying in the air as the bullets struck the ground just outside my car door. It was all occurring in slow motion. In front of me, Jacques frantically turned the wheel, hand over hand, spinning us around and giving me a clear view of a crater in the road created by the second grenade. That grenade would have destroyed our vehicle completely. Right then I felt the military officer's hand on the back of my neck. "Get down! Get down!" he yelled as he pushed my head toward the floor of the car.

As we hastily retreated in the direction from which we had just come, my heart sank. Equal to the terror of the last few minutes was my overwhelming sense of despair. Even before the military officer spoke, I knew what he was going to say. "We must go back. There is no way we can drive into Gitamara safely today. It's just too dangerous." To the driver, he added, "Let's take the boy back home."

As the officers loudly speculated that the attack had come from RPF fighters who had assumed the government vehicle was carrying Hutu officials, hot tears escaped my closed eyelids and flowed silently down my cheeks. But in a display of extraordinary self-control, I swallowed the scream that pressed against my clenched jaw and quivering lips. *Why are people trying to kill me? Is my family still safe in Gitamara? All I want is to see my mother's face!* I did not say these words out loud. Instead, they ricocheted in my head. One glance at the three men in the car told me they were still shaken by how close they had come to dying just moments before. They were obviously in no mood to entertain my questions.

Victor stared at me as I emerged from the car in front of the gate. "What happened?" he asked in disbelief. I walked by him in silence, leaving the young officer to explain to him what had just transpired. I headed to my room and crawled into my bed for the first time since leaving home that first day with my family. Soon my sobs echoed throughout the empty house.

Two days later I was presented with yet another opportunity to join my family in Gitamara. Francois and I were returning from a short walk early in the afternoon when we were approached by a young man I recognized. He was another one of those boys who from time to time had helped carry our purchases on market day. In the course of our brief conversation with him, Francois mentioned that I wanted to get to Gitamara but the men at the roadblocks would not let me pass by.

"The roadblocks are not a problem," the boy said confidently. "I can get you through. The men will think you are my little brother. Come, I will take you now." As an afterthought he added, "Your father is a good man. He has always been kind to me." I had no idea how he had come to know Papa, but I smiled appreciatively before running back to the house to get my bag. Minutes later I was saying goodbye to everyone at the house again. For the third time. As the boy and I headed off together down the road, I hoped it would be the last.

My companion had a gun, and he walked with purpose and confidence. I followed a few steps behind him. I was acutely aware that the young man with whom I walked was now a murderer who had taken the lives of many of my Tutsi neighbors. I tried to block that thought from my mind and to focus instead on a single goal—rejoining my family. As my companion had promised, we were waved through the first few roadblocks without incident. He led me along a different route than the one I had taken with my mother and sisters, and to my relief, we did not encounter the soldier who had ordered me out of the car. With each roadblock we passed, I allowed myself to feel a little more hope.

We had been walking for about an hour when we reached the fourth roadblock. Suddenly a sharp, high-pitched voice called out loudly, "Tutsi, Tutsi!" and I was startled to find a rifle pointing directly at my chest. I froze. My traveling companion immediately stepped between me and the gun. "No!" he shouted. "I know him. He is Hutu. The man I work for is Hutu, and this is his son." The man at the roadblock was not convinced. "Move! Or I will shoot both of you," he yelled. "How is this Tutsi still alive? Where was he hiding?"

I glanced around at the group of men loitering at the roadblock. Some looked up when the commotion started but soon turned back to what they had been doing before. Several didn't even glance our way. Someone was threatening to kill me *and* a fellow member of their militia, but no one seemed to be bothered. I swallowed hard. Waves of cramping pain squeezed my stomach as I realized that no one in the vicinity cared whether I lived or died. It was as if to them, I was no longer a human being.

For several tense seconds, my traveling companion and the man at the roadblock stared at each other in silence. My companion had raised his rifle immediately in response to the threat, but each man seemed reluctant to be the first to squeeze the trigger. Out of the corner of my eye, I noticed movement. One of the men who had been seated a few meters away sauntered over to where the three of us were standing. He seemed to be a little older than the others. He eyed me suspiciously before turning his attention to the two gunmen. The three argued loudly for about a minute, the newcomer trying to mediate the conflict, which was on the verge of erupting into gunfire. Both men eventually lowered their guns but continued to glare menacingly at each other as the mediator waved us through the roadblock, and we continued down the road. Afraid to look back as we hurried away, I braced for the bullet I feared would soon pierce my spine.

As soon as we rounded a bend in the road, my companion stopped abruptly and turned to look at me. No one else was in sight. It was only then that I noticed his pupils were dilated and sweat drenched his face and the front of his shirt. "We cannot go on," he said weakly. "If we are confronted by others who also think you are a Tutsi, we may not be so lucky next time. They will kill you and me. I am so sorry, but I cannot protect you." He spoke quickly, his words tumbling out of his mouth. He then paused and examined my face intently before shaking his head and adding, "You look too much like your mother."

Feeling desperate as I watched the boy who had just saved my life run away from me, I knew there was nothing else to do but make my way home. I dared not go back through the roadblock we had just passed, so I skirted it by traveling through the bushes until I came to the road that ran past our compound, reasoning that any members of the Interahamwe I encountered there would likely recognize me from my daily walks with Victor and Francois. For the third time, I knocked on the gate to my compound, and Victor let me in. This time his face conveyed more sadness than surprise. The same was true for Francois and the others who came out to greet me yet again. I felt hopeless. *What next?* I asked myself. I could not envision a future.

That night the battle for Kigali seemed to rage with even greater intensity. Sleep was impossible. The moment I closed my eyes, the shooting and explosions would start all over again. It was the darkest season of my young life. Nothing made sense. One day I was almost blown to pieces by unknown assailants because I was Hutu. A few days later I was almost shot to death because I was Tutsi. Lawlessness ruled the streets. My house no longer felt like my home. *Home*, I decided, was wherever my family was located, but I had no way to get there.

CHAPTER 8
Through the Forest

"Wake up, Bosco! Wake up!" I opened my eyes to see Francois standing over me. "Put on your shoes," he instructed as he stuffed food into my bag.

"What's happening?" I asked sleepily. It was then that I noticed that Thomas, Victor, and Christophe had also gathered in the garage and each man was holding one or two bags. Chantal had returned to her home several days before. Handing my bag to me, Francois explained, "The city is burning. It is too dangerous to remain." He paused to put the remaining food items into his own bag before continuing. "Everyone is running away, Bosco. We must leave too."

We hurried across the grass to the back of the compound and exited single file through a small gate in the wall that separated the rear of the compound from the forest. It was pitch black. I could barely make out the trees in front of us. A sudden barrage of explosions in the distance behind us caused me to glance over my shoulder. My house was a ghostly silhouette against a fiery red and orange sky. For years afterward that final view of my childhood home would remain indelibly engraved in my mind.

I soon realized we were not alone. Large numbers of people moved like shadows to my left and right. They moved swiftly, silently, and in the same direction. After a few minutes of trudging through the brush, I turned to ask Francois where we were going, but I could not find him. In fact, I could not see Victor, Christophe, or Thomas either. There were people all around me, but I couldn't make out anyone's face. Everyone was in a hurry. Rather than trying to find my companions in the dark, I decided to just keep moving forward. *When the sun comes up, I will find them,* I told myself. And so throughout that first night in the forest, I walked alone among hundreds of strangers. I ran when they ran, walked when they walked, and finally, as the sun began to rise, I sat down to rest when those around me sat.

It was only then that I realized the extent of this massive migration. For as far as my eyes could see, there were people—men, women, and children—as well as cows, pigs, and goats intermingled with the crowd. I knew then that I might never find Francois and the others among the great mass of people. I also noticed that sprinkled among the civilians were armed Interahamwe and government soldiers in uniform.

As the day wore on, everyone moved in one accord—sometimes running, sometimes walking, but always moving. The running was usually precipitated by bursts of gunfire or rockets that streaked low across the sky and detonated randomly all around us. A few landed near to me, but most exploded at a distance. I knew people were being injured or killed by these projectiles, but the crowd was so thick that I was shielded from seeing the dead. I had no idea where we were going or who was trying to kill us.

The next time we stopped to rest, I sat by myself in a small clearing. As I observed those around me, I bit into one of the roasted sweet potatoes that Francois had carefully wrapped and put in my bag. There was an eerie silence. Many people sat in what appeared to be family groups, but they did not speak to each other. Rather, they ate while staring blankly at nothing discernable. There were also quite a few who sat alone like me. Some people walked among the seated groups as if searching for someone. I considered looking for Francois and Victor, but I was too exhausted. Plus, it was unlikely that I would find them, I decided. There were just too many people.

I also thought about my cousin Thomas. I did not have a close relationship with him because he was more than seven years older than me, and he was usually busy with his studies or working for my father. But he was family, and he would have been a welcome sight at that moment. Family. As close as I was to my parents and siblings, I had never developed a close relationship with any members of my extended family. Yet in the midst of crisis, they all came to mind. Papa's family lived in a rural village to which I had traveled only once or twice. His mother would visit us often, however, and she would shower me with hugs, kisses, and edible treats. She was a great cook. She made it clear that she felt a special affection for me, her oldest grandson. Maman's family lived in a village that was even farther away. I can't recall ever going there. Her brother and sister would visit us regularly, however, and would always bring us freshly slaughtered chickens and eggs.

My parents may not have visited their childhood homes very often, but they provided financial support for many cousins, nieces, and nephews. Because of their generosity, these relatives were able to attend secondary schools and purchase school supplies and uniforms. *Papa and Maman are good people*, I thought. I missed them so much I could barely endure it.

Thinking about Maman and Papa and the rest of my family heightened my sense of isolation. I was surrounded by thousands of people, but I had never felt so alone. After eating, I stretched my body and leaned against the tree behind me. I must have dozed off for some time because I was woken up by the sound of a massive explosion about one hundred meters away to my right. Then came the unmistakable sound of gunfire. As if at the direction of an invisible conductor, everyone stood up in unison and began to run. Fathers and mothers picked up their young children, while others hastily stuffed half-eaten food and items of clothing into sacks before dashing off as fast as their legs could carry them and their load. Some simply left their belongings where they lay. The sun was already high in the sky, and I could now see clearly. It was as if the earth itself had become fluid and was undulating. But this was not a giant wave of water. It was men, women, children, and animals, propelled into a stampede by an unseen hand.

Eventually we all slowed to a walk. As I glanced around, I saw large numbers of Interahamwe and Hutu soldiers moving among the crowds. It slowly dawned on me that these men were hiding among us. It would be many more years before I understood that as the RPF had gained ground in the battle for Kigali, Hutu soldiers and Interahamwe had started to flee the city, taking cover by blending in among escaping civilians. Yet even without knowing this, I surmised that it was the presence of these soldiers and Interahamwe that attracted the bullets and the bombs that rained down on us intermittently. Nothing else made sense. After all, why would anyone want to kill *me*?

We plodded on for about two more hours before arriving at a stream. I could hear the voices of several men in the distance shouting that it was safe to stop and rest. I was grateful. It had been a while since we had last heard gunfire or bombs, and my throat was parched. I immediately began to drink, using my hands to scoop the water directly into my mouth. After quenching my thirst, I looked up to find that I had been drinking side by side with several farm animals. For a fleeting moment, I thought of Papa. Would he have reprimanded me for bringing shame to the family by sharing a drink with a cow? Perhaps not. My world had been turned upside down. I think he would have understood my desperation.

I got to my feet and looked around for a place to sit. Spying a log in the shade of a nearby tree, I moved in that direction. A young man with a rifle turned to look at me as I walked by. His eyes were red, and his demeanor suggested that somehow, here in the middle of the forest, he had secured enough alcohol to become drunk. His stare made me feel uncomfortable. Suddenly he yelled, "Tutsi spy! Tutsi spy!" I turned to see who he was referring to, and our eyes locked. Slowly he raised his gun and pointed it directly at my face.

Over the years I have often thought about the miraculous way in which Jesus saved my life that day—how he intervened in a split second. I do not know why he did that for me, but it serves as a constant reminder, even years later, that I dare not waste the extra time he has given me on the earth.

The miracle unfolded like this. Just as the drunken gunman was about to shoot me, we were both startled by a loud commotion. Out of nowhere came Francois, running and waving his arms like a maniac and shouting at the top of his lungs for my would-be killer to stop. I had not seen Francois for about twenty-four hours, so him finding me in the middle of a crowd of thousands *at just that moment* was nothing short of extraordinary. Francois came to a stop directly in front of me. As I had done at the roadblock days earlier, I hid my face between the shoulder blades of my protector.

Francois and the gunman yelled at each other for several moments, but I have no idea what they said. Fear had dulled my senses, and I was aware only of the fact that without a weapon, Francois was in no position to offer meaningful protection. Suddenly I heard a third voice, and I peered over Francois's shoulder to see who had joined the fray. It was Pierre, one of the men who had roamed the streets of Kigali daily in search of work. My father often hired him to do odd jobs at his stores, and both Francois and I had gotten to know him over the years. Relief washed over me at the sight of him now. Most importantly, he was holding a rifle.

Loudly, he joined with Francois in a desperate effort to convince my drunken attacker that I was not Tutsi and should be left alone. But my assailant was not convinced. If anything, it seemed the more Pierre spoke, the more agitated and aggressive he became. In a moment of panic, I made a split-second decision to bolt. Turning, I sprinted away faster than I ever had before, through the shallow stream and into the bush on the other side. I was deaf to everything but the pounding of my heart reverberating in my ears and the swish-swish of the leaves and small branches that scraped my legs and arms as I barreled through the undergrowth in my search for safety. I do not know how long I ran, but I doubt I could have maintained that speed for more than a few minutes. I eventually slowed to a jog, looking furtively behind me every few seconds to make sure I had not been followed. I relaxed when sometime later I caught up with another large group of several hundred people. They seemed to be heading toward the same unknown destination as the group I had just left behind. I made my way to the center of the crowd, reasoning that even if I had been followed, I would not easily be found in the midst of so many people.

If I had known then that it would be a long time before I would cross paths with Francois again, I would have become extremely sad. But I didn't know, so I trudged on, reassured that he was nearby and hopeful that I would see him soon. I would not discover until I spoke with Francois two years later that Pierre had shot my would-be killer when he attempted to chase after me. In doing so, Pierre had undoubtedly saved my life. The irony of what happened that day in the forest was not lost on me. That was the second time that a murderous member of the Interahamwe had protected me from a fellow member of their violent gang. My brain hurt as I tried to make sense of the madness that had engulfed us all.

PART THREE

No Longer Alone

CHAPTER 9

Exodus

I do not know how long I spent walking through the forest. It felt like a year, but it was likely not more than three or four days. Day and night were indistinguishable. We dozed at night, and we dozed during the day. We trudged on through the night, and we trudged on during the day. There was no structure or schedule. We moved when we were attacked, but we also stopped and started unpredictably or when ordered to do so over loudspeakers by the heavily armed military and Interahamwe who were all around us. After my earlier brush with death, I avoided these men at all costs. If one approached an area in which I was sitting or eating, I would move away as quickly and inconspicuously as possible. I desperately tried to shield my face, with its Tutsi-like features, from their view. My mother was beautiful, but sharing a resemblance to her could cost me my life.

No one engaged me in conversation, which was just as well. I did not want to talk, and everyone else seemed to feel the same way. We moved as a group, mostly in silence. The one constant during my time in the forest was my tears. I cried all the time. I cried mostly because of a deep loneliness that was impossible to dispel, especially at night. But I also cried because I knew that each time we were forced to run, whether in response to an explosion or to a command from the military, the people around me lost valuable personal possessions. There was simply no time to grab everything. Some even lost their children. I cried because each burst of gunfire likely meant that someone in the crush of bodies that surrounded me had lost his or her life. I cried because I was forced to subsist on raw arrowroot and dirty water. I was hungry all the time. Occasionally I would approach a woman who was cooking for her family over a wood fire and beg for a portion of their meal. I would then cry after eating the morsels they generously shared with me when I remembered the kitchen full of good food I had left behind at my house.

In addition to my intense loneliness, hunger, and fear of being murdered by the Interahamwe or incoming missiles, two incidents helped to completely erase the already rapidly diminishing sense of safety and security to which I still clung. The first was crossing the Nyabarongo River. The second happened near the end of our harrowing trek, when I unexpectedly encountered the body of a dead child.

It was very early in the morning when we arrived at the Nyabarongo River. The sun had not yet risen, and I was utterly exhausted from having walked for almost the entire night. Our group paused on the bank of the river to contemplate how to cross safely. Some took the opportunity to sit and rest, while others strolled along the riverbank trying to figure out the ideal location to venture into the chest-deep water. A few meters from where I stood was a makeshift bridge constructed of logs and branches that appeared to have been hastily assembled by a group that had crossed before us. It was in poor condition, having been trampled on by hundreds, if not thousands, of people ahead of us. Already partially submerged in the water, it appeared incapable of accommodating any additional weight.

After some discussion a small group of about eight or nine people joined hands and, without any warning, broke away from the rest of us and waded into the water. Slowly they made their way across the river in single file, each one clinging tightly to the hand of the person in front and behind. When the first person reached the other side, he scrambled up onto the grassy bank and turned to help the woman behind him. For the next few minutes, those on shore turned to help each member of the group climb out of the water until all were safely on the other side. While this was taking place, many of the cows began to swim across. Soon other groups of people began to form human chains, and the mass migration continued across the river.

I was petrified and stood rooted in place on the bank of the river. The river that flowed in front of me was quite unlike Lake Muhazi near my school. While the lake was still and clear, the flowing, opaque waters of the river filled me with fear. And for good reason. Three years before I had gone with a group of friends to a place called Nyabugogo. Although it was many kilometers away from where I stood, I knew that the very same Nyabarongo River that flowed in front of me now also flowed through that town. The memory of what I experienced during my first encounter with the river caused me to become immobilized.

Nyabugogo was about a thirty-minute walk from home, but neither my friends nor I had told our parents where we were going. On arriving at the river, I discovered that I was the only one in our group who did not know how to swim. When my friends realized this, they coaxed me to join them in the water and promised to teach me. But the lessons did not last long. Soon we were all playing in the river. I was so engrossed in the game that I did not realize that I was moving farther and farther away from the bank and into the deep. Without warning, the soft sand beneath my feet disappeared, and I began to sink. I frantically stretched my legs in a vain attempt to touch solid ground and find support for my body, but only water swirled beneath my toes. I knew I was drowning. I waved my arms in an attempt to attract my friends' attention. A weak scream escaped my lips just before I was completely submerged.

I later learned that a man who happened to be walking on the bridge that crossed over the river saw my predicament, jumped into the water, and pulled me to safety. He then administered CPR to my seemingly lifeless body until I regained consciousness and vomited up the river water that I had swallowed. I never did tell my parents or siblings about the incident. Now, as I stood on the banks of the Nyabarongo River for a second time, I did not want to enter its unwelcoming waters again.

I was jolted out of my memories by the touch of someone grasping my right hand. The woman who reached for me smiled and pulled me along to join a human chain of five or six others. As we neared the water's edge, someone behind me grabbed my left hand. Our chain grew in length as we waded into the cool water and began to make our way across. The water rose slowly from my knees to my hips and finally stopped level with my chest. Had it risen even one more centimeter, I think I would have screamed in full-blown panic. I still recall my immense relief when I was finally able to lie down in the grass on the other side of the river and turn my face toward the warm rays of the morning sun.

I am not sure when the second traumatic incident occurred. It may have been later that same day or perhaps the next. We were walking through a meadow where the terrain was flat, with only a few trees. Military vehicles moved through the area easily. In the distance I noticed a small group of people standing in a semicircle. They were waving their arms and seemed quite distraught. Curious, I approached the group to hear what they were saying. As I drew near, I saw the child. He was lying on his stomach with his face obscured. The skin on his back and limbs was partially peeled off. The onlookers were debating what had happened to him. Some claimed that a military jeep had accidentally hit the young child. Others said he had been trampled during a human stampede triggered by an exploding rocket. It was the first time I had ever seen a dead body, and it scared me. Where were this child's parents? Did they even know he was dead? Could that happen to me? If I died out here, who would know? I walked away, crying as much for myself as for that little boy.

During those days in the forest, I would sometimes think about God. Having spent so many Sundays throughout my childhood in our Catholic church, I had committed the Lord's Prayer and the Rosary to memory a long time ago. In the forest I would often recite both. It was the only way I knew to connect with God, and I desperately wanted to feel his presence and to draw closer to him. I also prayed because it reminded me of life before the genocide began. Here in the forest, I could no longer brush my teeth, shower, or sit down to a delicious breakfast served by Christophe. The things that had given structure to my life—waking up in a comfortable bed, going to class, doing homework, and eating dinner—were no more. All had been replaced by a seemingly endless cycle of walking, running, and briefly resting in the grass in the shadow of tall trees or thick bushes. This new routine made absolutely no sense to me. I did not know where we were going or why. I yearned for a time when there would be no shooting and for a place where I could rest in comfort. But most of all, I desperately wanted to see my family and feel my mother's embrace.

I remember the moment I learned we were heading to Ruhengeri. I overheard a conversation between two soldiers, and for the first time since being forced to abandon my home, I experienced a rush of hope. We had family friends in Ruhengeri, a city in the north of Rwanda that I had visited multiple times. I had fond memories of the majestic highlands that towered over the area and were home to Rwanda's famous mountain gorillas. I had spent many hours observing this scenery from the porch of the large home of our friends.

My father referred to the patriarch of the large, wealthy family who lived in Ruhengeri as Patrick, but I do not believe that was his real name. Regardless, my siblings and I called him Mr. Patrick. My father would buy the produce from Mr. Patrick's farms and then distribute the truckloads of potatoes, maize, beans, and other items throughout Kigali and beyond. The children in the Patrick family ranged from a five-year-old to teenagers to those in their early twenties. Though I was never quite sure exactly how many children lived on the property, I knew that several were within two years of my age, which meant there was always someone with whom I could play when I visited.

Every year during the summer holidays, my parents would send me to visit the Patricks for two weeks. Some of my fondest childhood memories were created during my time in Ruhengeri. Often, Mr. Patrick and a couple of his sons would pick me up in Kigali and we would make the two-and-a-half-hour drive together to their home. On the way we would pass many farms, and as the tall mountains would come into view, I would become excited. Farming was big business in the area, and many people had moved there for work. Huge, bustling warehouses filled with recently harvested crops were located throughout the community.

Because of the higher elevation, the air in Ruhengeri was much cooler than in Kigali. I loved that I could run and play there without getting hot and sweaty. The houses were built far apart from each other, and compounds were without the high walls that were typical in my own neighborhood. Around the perimeter of the Patricks' property, trees and flowers had been strategically planted. I enjoyed the wide-open atmosphere of the compound, and I felt free there.

Mealtime in the Patrick home was so interesting. I was always amazed at the amount of food that was served and the fact that no matter how much we ate, there were always leftovers. We could never finish the food on the table. The Patricks had household servants who, together with the older children, would bring the food from the kitchen and serve everyone. Whereas in my home I did no household chores, the Patrick children were required to complete certain household tasks. I was not allowed to even step in the kitchen at my house, but at the Patricks' house, everybody helped out. I really enjoyed being a part of the organized chaos of laughter, exuberant chatter, and nonstop movement that was on display at every meal.

Whenever I stayed with the Patricks, as soon as the sun came up, I would gulp down my breakfast and race out to play in the yard or walk to the nearby town. I loved being able to go wherever I wanted to with the other children. I even enjoyed doing chores. Although there was running water in the faucets in their home, the compound had several tanks in which extra water was stored. Given the size of the family, plus the number of household servants, it was essential for them to keep the tanks filled with water at all times. So every day I would go with some of the children to a communal well, which was about a ten-minute walk from the house. We would fill our buckets with water and return home to dump the water we had collected into one of the tanks at the back of the compound. In this way, the tank was continually replenished with both rainwater and well water.

There was usually a line of people waiting to fill their buckets at the community well. I would play and chat with the other children as we waited, which made the chore feel like fun rather than work. Another task that was more pleasurable than burdensome was doing the laundry. Not far from the well was a small body of water—I believe it was a man-made river—where we washed our clothes. After washing, we would put our clothes on the grass and rocks to dry and play a multitude of games as we waited.

A few of the Patrick children had stayed overnight at our house in Kigali, usually on occasions when they came to the city to see a doctor or when Mr. Patrick brought them along on one of his business trips. However, most of the children had never traveled to the city. They were very curious about life in Kigali, and I enjoyed describing the city to them and telling them about my siblings. My bond with the Patrick family had grown stronger every year. I loved them, and they showed their affection for me by welcoming me warmly and folding me into their large family each summer.

Curiously, I was the only one of my siblings who spent extended periods of time with the Patricks in Ruhengeri. I do not know why my sisters or brothers never came with me. It did not occur to me to ask my parents why, nor do I recall any of my siblings ever expressing any interest in going with me. Given the future that awaited me, I am convinced it was God's plan for me to develop a strong relationship with that specific family. Only he could have known the role they would later play in saving my life and in securing my future.

Now, as I neared Ruhengeri with the crowd of travelers, my steps began to quicken. "I will make my way to the Patrick compound, and they will help me," I whispered to myself. As I had avoided all conversation in the past few days, it was strange to hear my own voice out loud. But the sound energized and motivated me. Suddenly, the roar of a jeep interrupted my thoughts, and I looked up to see the military officer whom my father had sent to rescue me driving past. I ran toward the jeep, waving my hands. As I approached the vehicle, I noticed immediately that he was drunk. So drunk, in fact, that I doubt he even recognized me. I tried to speak to him, but his glassy eyes stared right through me as his jeep rolled by. My heart sank. It was already late in the evening, so I decided to join a small group of people who had settled down in the grass for the night.

The next morning everything changed. The military official and his bodyguards, who had ignored me the evening before, had apparently parked nearby overnight. Soon after waking up, I again encountered them on the road. The men were sober now, and the officer greeted me enthusiastically when I approached him the second time. They made room for me in their jeep, and I quickly climbed in, my words tumbling out eagerly as I explained where I was going.

About fifteen minutes later, we pulled into Ruhengeri. Thousands of people had already emerged from the forests and now clogged the roadways and buildings in the town. It seemed as if every square inch was overrun with people. I barely recognized the community. Nevertheless, I was able to direct the driver to the Patrick family's compound. Though we were forced to drive very slowly, we eventually arrived at my destination. As I gazed at the house where I had spent so many happy summers, I was overcome with emotion, and my heart beat rapidly. I could hardly believe I had survived the forest and made it to my second home.

CHAPTER 10
Road to Zaire

"Bosco! What are you doing here? Where are your parents?" Mr. Patrick stared at me wide-eyed as I stood at the door to his palatial home. Only a sob escaped my lips. "How did you get here?" He persisted. Failing to get a response from me, he turned to the men in the jeep for answers.

As the military officer began to explain, I looked behind Mr. Patrick into the large foyer that led to the living room. I was surprised to see several of the children and household servants busily packing boxes and bags with food and an assortment of other items, as if they were preparing for a trip. *Where could they possibly be going at a time like this?* I asked myself.

After a brief exchange with Mr. Patrick, the men returned to their jeep and drove off. As they disappeared down the road, it occurred to me that the military officer had not returned the money that he still owed me. I would never see him again, nor would I ever get the money Papa had sent for me. I subsequently learned that later that very night, the officer got drunk and was seriously injured in a bar fight in town. Some rumors had it that he had been killed. But I didn't care about the money he owed me. It could not help me locate my family or return me to the life I once knew. If money could do neither of those things, then what was the point in having it?

As the men left, Mr. Patrick followed me into the foyer, where I had wandered. "You need a bath and a good meal," he observed. "Go and bathe yourself, and tell one of the boys to give you some clean clothes. I'll also tell the cook to fix you something to eat." I thanked him and turned to go. But before I could take a step, he put his arm gently on my shoulder. "Don't worry, Bosco," he said softly. "Your home is with us for now. Once the war is over, I promise I will help you to find your parents." I nodded as a lump slowly and painfully formed in my throat and stinging tears burned the back of my eyes.

The next two days passed in a whirlwind of activity. Fighting between the Hutu-backed Rwandan military and the Tutsi-backed RPF for control of the country was escalating. Many of the Hutu civilians in Ruhengeri and elsewhere feared that an RPF victory would result in retaliatory violence against them because of the Hutus' brutality toward the Tutsis around the country. Fearing this possibility, the Patrick family and hundreds of other Hutu families decided it was best to leave Rwanda and to return only when things settled down.

By the time I had arrived at the Patrick home, preparations for the move to the neighboring country of Zaire were already well underway. Everyone helped to pack and load the large truck that was parked in the driveway. It was an awesome spectacle. Everything was conducted in an orderly fashion, and everyone worked together smoothly. Even the youngest children seemed to know exactly what was expected of them and completed their tasks with minimum guidance.

I stayed in Ruhengeri for two nights. As I settled between the clean sheets on the final night, the soft mattress enveloped my entire body. How I had missed this simple pleasure! I had lived like an animal in the forest—sleeping on the hard earth, relieving myself in the bushes, digging up roots for food. Now, with my hunger satiated and my washed body stretched out on a bed, I began to reclaim my humanity. As my mind meandered from one thought to the next, a very sobering realization came to me: if I had arrived in Ruhengeri just two days later than I had, the Patrick family would have left town without me. What would have happened to me then? Before drifting off to sleep, I whispered the shortest, yet most sincerely felt prayer I had ever prayed: "Thank you, Jesus."

On the day of our planned departure, I climbed with most of the other family members on top of the goods in the back of the truck and settled in for the drive to Zaire. Mr. Patrick's oldest son, Gael, was at the wheel of the truck. A smaller number of people loaded themselves into the family's pickup truck, which was similarly laden with food and household items. Left behind were the servants and one or two adult family members who chose to remain on the property to keep an eye on things.

Members of the Interahamwe were everywhere, and even Mr. Patrick, with all his wealth and influence, was at their mercy. The danger was very real. In fact, before we had pulled out of the compound, Mr. Patrick had taken me aside, and in a quiet yet firm voice issued the following instruction: "Hide your face as best you can, Bosco, especially at the roadblocks. It will be best if you stay covered until we get to a place where there is less traffic and fewer people on the roads. I cannot prove that you are my son, and I do not want the Interahamwe to think you are a Tutsi who is trying to escape." He concluded with a blunt but honest assessment of the danger, "If they see you, they may pull you off the truck and kill you." Because of my recent experience in the forest, I knew he was speaking the truth and quickly nodded in agreement. Moments later our two vehicles, laden with people, food, and other supplies, pulled out of the driveway and joined the throngs heading to Zaire.

Under normal circumstances the drive from Mr. Patrick's house to the border would have taken less than an hour. But there was nothing normal about this journey. The trip took us an entire day because the road was jammed with trucks and cars, as well as people traveling on foot and carrying their possessions or pushing carts filled with personal items. Scores of young boys and men ushered small herds of animals toward the border, adding to the chaos. It was hot in the back of Mr. Patrick's truck, but I was otherwise fairly comfortable. I lay down on sacks of maize, beans, sugar, and clothes, a thin, opaque cotton sheet covering my body.

Our truck had been used for carrying heavy loads of stones and sand before being conscripted to carry food and people. The vehicle was long and wide, with ten very large tires, each of which was almost my height. As a result, those of us in the back were perched high above street level, partially obscured from the view of those walking below us. I was also surrounded by six or seven of Mr. Patrick's children, their bodies effectively blocking me from the prying gazes of passersby and providing me with an extra measure of protection.

Even so, what I dreaded most during that long day were the frequent roadblocks. Men with guns would jump up on the side of the truck and take a cursory glance into the back. Mr. Patrick's children would greet them loudly and enthusiastically: "Hello! We are all family back here! Our big brother is driving, and our father is in the vehicle in front of us." They would then animatedly point ahead to the lead vehicle in an attempt to distract the men. The children all understood that I needed to remain hidden, and one or two of them would sit on top of me when we approached the barriers just to make sure I wouldn't be seen.

At a few of these roadblocks, I overheard the men demanding identification from our driver, Gael. It reminded me that I had little else besides my school identification card. When I had run from my house in Kigali that fateful night, I believed I would be returning home in a day or two. In addition to food, I had packed a few personal items like photos, shoes, and clothes. But as hours stretched into days in the forest, I had discarded these items in an effort to lighten my load. By the time I reached the Patrick home, my bag was almost empty. I had focused on surviving, not on preserving my belongings. Now I was getting ready to cross from Rwanda into Zaire with little more than the clothes on my back.

We arrived in Zaire late in the evening. The border was wide-open to the throngs moving in, and from my perspective, but for the presence of Zairean military personnel, it was difficult to determine where one country ended and the other began. We stayed overnight in the town of Goma in an empty building near a small airstrip. I think the building may have been a small store that belonged to someone with whom Mr. Patrick had done business in the past. What mattered most to me, however, was that we had four sturdy walls around us and a roof to protect us from the elements. Compared to what I had endured recently, it was luxurious. Thankfully, we were also far away from the crowds that had surrounded us all day.

Before settling down for the night, I helped two of Mr. Patrick's teenage sons, William and Benjamin, to pull a few mattresses out of the pickup truck. We brought them into the building and dropped them on the floor. Immediately several of the younger children stretched out on top of them. A few minutes later, Mr. Patrick's wife,

Miss Alice, and their two oldest daughters, Olive and Honorine, unwrapped potatoes, corn, and pieces of meat that had been cooked at home that morning. They laid out the humble feast on a lone table in the center of the room. There was little conversation as we ate. We were all exhausted. After eating, we each wrapped ourselves in one of the many blankets the household servants had packed, lay down on the floor, and promptly fell asleep. All of us, that is, except Mr. Patrick's oldest sons, Gael and Jean-Claude. He had instructed them to sleep outside in the vehicles to keep an eye on our belongings and hopefully deter any would-be robbers.

The next morning, as we ate a simple breakfast of potatoes and fruit, Mr. Patrick announced his plan. "We will not be staying here in Goma," he said. "There are too many refugees in this area. It is much too crowded and dirty. There are also diseases spreading and killing people in the refugee camps." He paused and looked at the youngest children, who were listening to him intently, before adding, "And a lot of very bad things are happening in the camps." It was clear to me that he was using less graphic and disturbing language than he had originally intended because he did not want to frighten his younger children. "So we will keep driving today," he continued. "A friend of mine has given us permission to rent his house in a town called Ruanguba. It is to the north, only a few hours away." Then, glancing at me, he added with a reassuring smile, "The Interahamwe and others in the refugee camp will not follow us there. It will be peaceful and safe." I breathed a sigh of relief. I desperately wanted to get as far away as possible from the crowds that had surrounded us on the drive to Goma.

The drive to Ruanguba was far more enjoyable than our journey the day before. I was finally able to shed my covering and sit on top of the cargo without fear of being discovered. And although there were still long periods of silence, conversation flowed more freely among the children in the truck. The older teens were curious as to why I was not with my own family. I did not feel like reciting the entire story, so I simply told them that I had been accidentally separated from my parents during the fighting in Kigali. "But when this fighting is over, I will find them, or they will find me," I said, trying to sound confident. The Patrick children were sad, too, and they shared their own concerns with me. The younger ones were puzzled and upset by the need to flee so suddenly, and the older ones wondered out loud when, if ever, they would be able to return home and see their friends again.

Our underlying anxiety was heightened moments later when we were forced to stop because Mr. Patrick had developed a nosebleed. Blood stained his shirt and pants and soaked through the handkerchiefs that had been shoved into his hands by those sitting closest to him in the pickup truck. It was a terrifying sight, and several of the younger children began to cry. "Is Papa going to die?" whispered one of his young daughters. I reassured her as best I could that he would be fine.

The bleeding continued on and off for almost the entire day. I think Mr. Patrick's nosebleed was due to stress. He was responsible for the safety of his entire family, and we were in a foreign country with limited access to his resources. His burden was no doubt tremendous, and I feared for his well-being. What would happen to all of us if he became really ill? My own stress level went sky-high at the thought. Everything about my life seemed so insecure. There was nothing firm or sure to which I could cling.

Fortunately, the spectacular beauty of the scenery that surrounded us as we drove north lifted our spirits, and I stood up in the back of the truck in an effort to take it all in. The traffic had thinned out considerably, and there were no other vehicles behind or in front of us when we entered a lush, sparsely populated forest. A few scattered farms dotted the landscape, but what completely enthralled us was the wildlife—gazelles, antelopes, monkeys, elephants, baboons, and more species of birds than we could count. I could feel the cool breeze and warm sunshine on my face as we sped along, and for a few glorious moments, I allowed myself to imagine that I was on vacation. And then it happened. I smiled for the very first time since being separated from my mother and sisters. It felt awkward, even strange, but I could not resist the urge as I watched the antics of the monkeys in the trees overhead. Even more thrilling was when we stopped for lunch and a few of them decided to drop by. They approached us tentatively at first but grew bolder when they realized we were willing to share our bananas with them. This was a completely new experience for me and a welcome distraction from all that had gone wrong in my life.

We arrived in Ruanguba just as the sun was setting. The cloud of despondency that had dissipated during our ride through the forest had claimed us once again during the last few kilometers of our journey. Our conversations had gradually come to a halt. While some dozed, the rest of us stared vacantly into the distance, lost in our own thoughts as the truck bounced along the uneven road toward our destination. This was not the joyful Patrick family I had known. Though I believed that my anguish was greater than theirs, I knew we all longed for a return to normalcy that seemed more elusive with each passing kilometer.

Our new home was a large concrete house surrounded by a sprawling yard. It was owned by an Anglican bishop who had recently moved away. Mr. Patrick unlocked the front door to reveal a well-furnished living room, multiple bedrooms, an enormous dining room, and a spacious kitchen. The house was more than adequate to accommodate all of us comfortably.

I could scarcely believe our good fortune as I thought back to the squalor of the refugee camps that we had passed along our way. Without a doubt Mr. Patrick was very well-connected to some important people, and they were willing to help him during this time of crisis and upheaval.

With so many helpers, the process of unloading the truck and sorting and storing food, clothes, personal items, and an assortment of household articles took a surprisingly short amount of time. Once everything was neatly put away, we sat down to a simple supper that had been hurriedly prepared by Miss Alice. After supper we figured out bedroom assignments. Soon the house became quiet as, one by one, we fell asleep.

So began my new life in Zaire. The transition was hard. In the days that followed, I felt unmoored, detached from everything that was familiar to me. I was in a new country with a new family. Not even the clothes on my back or shoes on my feet were mine. My sense of loss was profound, and many times I seriously considered suicide. The feeling of being completely alone and adrift in a big, unpredictable, and dangerous world engulfed me. Where could I put this pain, fear, and anger that threatened to make my brain explode and my heart burst? The emotions were inescapable and unrelenting. I believed that I was losing my mind. It was in those tortured moments that the dark nothingness that I imagined death to be seemed most attractive. Life had lost its meaning. Could death be any worse? Watching the Patrick children interact with each other and their parents was intensely painful because it served as a constant reminder that I had no idea whether my own family was dead or alive. I refused to eat more than a mouthful of food at each meal, and I cried morning and evening.

One day, about two weeks after we had arrived at our new home, one of Mr. Patrick's older female relatives, whom we all called Nana, sat me down. Staring intently into my eyes, she said without preamble, "You are going to die of hunger, Bosco." After a brief pause, she continued slowly, "I know you miss your family. But if you die now, you will not be able to help us look for them. And you will not be here when we find them. How will that make them feel?" Her demeanor was firm yet comforting, and her simple logic was convincing. Sensing that she had penetrated the darkness that engulfed me, she smiled. "I know how you feel," she assured me. "When I was a child, I came to live with Mr. Patrick's family because my own parents had died. I was sad at first, but I realized that even though I was an orphan, I had to get on with my own life and I could not mourn forever." With that, she hugged me and left me alone to think about what she had said.

That moment with Nana was a turning point. I began to think less of suicide and tried to cultivate hope. Nana also kept an eye on me. She made sure I ate and went out of her way to cheer me up when I was sad. Her efforts were not always successful. Periodic bouts of depression continued to haunt me for a long time. But I am convinced that without her persistent, intentional intervention, I may very well have taken my own life.

Nana's statement also reminded me to follow up with Mr. Patrick regarding his promise. "We must wait a little longer before we go looking for your parents, Bosco," he told me. "Things are still very chaotic in the refugee camps, and cholera is spreading rapidly. It is not safe to go there right now. We will wait a few more months, and then we will visit the camps. If your parents are there, we will find them." Mr. Patrick's tone was confident. I trusted him, and I believed that I would be reunited with my family. The only question was, *when?*

CHAPTER 11
The Four Laws

In the weeks following our arrival in Zaire, Nana and Mr. Patrick continued to watch over me and give me hope—an emotion so powerful that it would lift me from the pits of despair into which I repeatedly fell. The promise of being able to search for my parents was a powerful antidote to the darkness that threatened to overwhelm me. Had it not been for both Nana and Mr. Patrick, I might not have survived.

My friendships with William, Benjamin, and the other children also contributed to my emotional and psychological well-being. I would often escape my persistent sadness by participating enthusiastically in whatever game the other children were playing. This would work for a while, but then, at an unpredictable moment—often while I was in the very act of laughing or kicking a soccer ball—a tidal wave of sorrow would crash over me. Without a word to the others, I would turn and run away in a desperate attempt to be alone with my grief. Those left behind would exchange bewildered glances and draw close together to whisper questions about why I had left so abruptly. But they had no answers, and eventually they would shrug their shoulders and go back to playing their game.

About a month after arriving in Ruanguba, we began attending our new school. I do not remember the date, but I know it was before my fifteenth birthday in September 1994. I am not sure who made the decision, but I had to repeat grade seven, perhaps because I had not completed the school year before being forced to flee Rwanda. The Patrick children who were assigned to grades seven through twelve attended the same secondary school, while the younger ones attended elementary school together.

Most mornings it was wet and cold when we left home to begin our twenty-five-minute walk to school. The route took us over a flimsy wooden pedestrian bridge, and I would look warily at the waters swirling below as I hurried across. The school, which had been established by the local Baptist Mission, was perched high on a hill overlooking the small but busy town of Ruanguba with its community hospital, small government buildings, several shops, and a collection of single-story buildings that housed Baptist pastors and missionaries, as well as their families. Nearby a similar cluster of buildings housed the Catholic mission where priests and nuns worshipped and served the community.

On the outskirts of town stood one of the large cinchona forests that were common throughout the eastern region of Zaire. Many of Ruanguba's residents worked in the forest. The bark of the towering Cinchona trees contains quinine, a drug that treats malaria. To meet the great demand for quinine in Zaire and elsewhere in Africa, men worked tirelessly to strip the tree bark with the aid of machines. Trucks would then transport the bark elsewhere for further processing. It was convenient having the forest nearby for personal reasons. Whenever we felt sick, we would take a walk down one of the trails and cut off a little piece of tree bark. Chewing the bark released an intensely bitter substance that would cause us to become drowsy. After a good night's sleep, we would always wake up feeling better, yet even now, years later, the memory of that bitter taste still puts my teeth on edge.

I welcomed the routine of going to school because it allowed me to focus on something other than my absent family. During the day my teachers kept my mind occupied with learning, and in the evenings, I would immerse myself in homework and reading. Thanks to the power generated by a nearby river, we had electricity, so our evening activities were not curtailed in any way. The most important thing I did every night before going to bed was listen to the radio. I would eagerly tune in to one main station on which the announcer read the names of people who were looking for loved ones who might be in the refugee camps. He would also read the names of people who were in the refugee camps, who wanted to alert loved ones to their specific location. This recitation of names would last for almost two hours, and I would listen intently, hoping to hear a name I recognized. I was disappointed every time.

When that broadcast ended, I would then tune in to the British Broadcasting Corporation's radio station to catch up on world news, as well as news from each of the refugee camps. Convinced that my family was in one of these camps, I was concerned about reports of diseases, outbreaks of violence, and other distressing developments within the camps.

On the weekends I spent hours writing letters to various international organizations, such as the United Nations High Commission for Refugees (UNHCR), International Red Cross, and World Food Programme (WFP), all of which had a presence in the refugee camps. I would describe my family and provide their names, hoping that someone would recognize them. The response was always the same: no one knew my family or where they might be. Although these efforts yielded no positive outcomes, I continued to write letters and listen to the radio for months. I felt less helpless when I actively tried to find Papa and Maman.

A few weeks after arriving at my new school, I organized a dance group with about eight or nine other students. The radio provided the loud, energetic music to which we gyrated with abandon. We danced to rumba and Lingala—the most popular music in Zaire during the mid-1990s. These dances required physical strength and stamina, and as I listened to the cadence and beat of each song and willed my entire body to execute a myriad of quick, rhythmic moves, I was temporarily transported beyond the reach of the emotional pain that hounded me every day. Dancing became a form of therapy that left me drenched in sweat, utterly exhausted, acutely aware of my heartbeat, and extremely happy. While Nana tended to my physical needs with food and Mr. Patrick shored me up emotionally with the promise of finding my family, the music and dance of my newly adopted country nurtured my soul in a way that nothing else did.

Toward the end of our first year in Zaire, Mr. Patrick made several important decisions that would affect every member of the family. The genocide in Rwanda had ended a couple of months after our exodus with the toppling of the Hutu-led government by the Tutsi-led RPF. The political situation had become more stable, and many Rwandan refugees, including Mr. Patrick, began to consider returning home. He was markedly encouraged by reports from home that the house in Ruhengeri was secure, the household servants were well, and it was safe to return.

Cautious by nature, Mr. Patrick nevertheless decided that it was best for the family to be strategically dispersed rather than for everyone to return to Rwanda all at once. So in the middle of 1995, Mr. Patrick sent his wife and the younger children to live in Goma, close to the Rwandan border, in preparation for their eventual return to Ruhengeri. We teenagers were told to remain in Ruanguba and to continue to attend our high school for another year. Those who had already graduated he sent to Kenya to work and to attend university there. In this carefully planned manner, Mr. Patrick sought to protect and provide for his very large family, from the oldest to the youngest.

Although I did not think about it at the time, I later wondered how Mr. Patrick, a refugee, was able to generate the resources necessary to implement this intricate and expensive plan for his large family. While he did not discuss his personal finances with me, I assume that his farming and food distribution businesses in Rwanda must have continued to successfully operate during his absence. The big truck that had transported us and our belongings out of Rwanda had also generated significant income for the family. Mr. Patrick was able to secure a contract that allowed him to distribute food from the various international aid organizations to the refugee camps in Zaire because he owned that large truck.

As a teenager without parents, belongings, or money, I was extremely fortunate to have connected with the Patrick family. Not only were they willing to take care of me, but they had the means to do so as well. I thanked God for them then, and, even today, I still marvel at the crucial role they played in ensuring my survival.

During the summer between grade seven and grade eight, Mr. Patrick fulfilled his promise to begin looking for my parents. He and I went to several refugee camps near Goma and in the surrounding areas. But it was all to no avail. There was no record of my parents or of any of my siblings anywhere. The refugee camps were teeming with thousands of people, and I would survey the wide expanse of humanity with squinted eyes, imagining that my parents were there somewhere but hidden from view. The international officials assured us, however, that was not the case. "If your parents' names are not on our list, it is because they are not here," they insisted. "Everyone has been registered." Following each of these visits, I would return home to Ruanguba, crushed with disappointment.

Just before school resumed in the latter half of 1995, Mr. Patrick sent those of us who were to remain in Ruanguba to live in a hostel that was practically next door to the high school. The house where we had lived for the past year was much too large and the upkeep too expensive for our shrinking household. Gael and Olive, Mr. Patrick's oldest son and daughter, moved with us to the hostel to help care for us and to provide supervision, while Mr. Patrick traveled back and forth between us and the rest of the family in Goma.

The search for my own family continued, but only on weekends after I returned to school to start grade eight. Sometimes Mr. Patrick would accompany me, but there were times when I went alone because he was with his family in Goma. Before leaving Ruanguba, he would always give me money for food and to pay for transportation to the camps. On several Saturday mornings, I rose early and set out alone for a camp close enough that I could visit and then return to the hostel the same day.

I had recently turned sixteen years old, and my demeanor was solemn. My one, all-consuming goal was to find my family. Until I did, there was nothing to smile about. Because I was both quiet and serious, many people assumed I was much older. This proved helpful in my interactions with personnel at the refugee camps. Having already made many trips with Mr. Patrick throughout the area during the summer, I knew my way around via the various minivan and trucking routes that crisscrossed the area. I was also familiar with the process of requesting information from the appropriate officials at the camps. And although my hope waned with each passing week, I still looked forward to these visits with great anticipation. *Maybe this is the weekend I will find my family*, I would tell myself before falling asleep each night.

There had been ample opportunities for me to attend church in Ruanguba once we arrived and settled into a routine. But I chose to ignore the mostly Baptist and Catholic churches in the community. Prior to fleeing Kigali, I had gone to church almost every Sunday, most often with my mother. In Ruanguba, however, I feared that entering a church building would stir memories of Maman. Those memories would then have released a familiar ache—an ache that would start in the pit of my stomach before radiating to every inch of my body. That sealed it. There would be no more church for me. Church and Maman were too inextricably and painfully intertwined in my mind and heart.

To be clear, while I avoided church, I did not reject God. In fact, while fleeing Kigali through the forest, I often recited the prayers that I had memorized, as well as the hymns I had once sung. Indeed, those early experiences in church served me well during that horrendous time. I had what I now call "head knowledge" of God. I believed that he could protect me, and I prayed that he would. I received comfort in doing that. Unlike so many who grow to hate God or who reject religion when bad things happen to them, I still viewed God with reverence and respect. But he was a distant deity. Not one whom I knew well or who I believed knew me very well. Not one who I believed would respond to my specific request for a heavenly intervention in my circumstances. I also had a lot of questions I wanted to ask him. Questions like "Why am I suffering? Why are other children not experiencing the pain that I am going through?" But I naively believed it would have been disrespectful to ask God these questions, so I kept them to myself.

It was against this religious backdrop that my friend Kwima asked me the most important question I had ever been asked in my life: "Bosco, do you know Jesus?" The question startled me. School had ended for the day, and I was sitting alone in an empty classroom doing my homework. Although we were not close friends, Kwima and I sometimes chatted together while we ate our lunch. Now he stood leaning against the door, hands in his pockets, his eyes peering intently into mine. Without waiting for me to answer, Kwima continued, "You need Jesus, Bosco. He is the only one who can help you in your situation."

Years later I would look back in wonder at the way in which Kwima's simple question, followed by his astute observation, launched me on a new path toward a glorious destiny that I would not have thought possible, given my circumstances and emotional condition at that time. I did not realize it then, but my life was about to be transformed from hopeless to hopeful. But at that moment, I could only stare at him. What kind of question was that? Did he want to know if I believed in God? Or if I went to church? Or said my prayers? But Kwima had not asked me about any of that. His question was entirely different. He was not interested in knowing if I was "religious." Rather, he wanted to know if I was in a personal *relationship* with Jesus. I was puzzled. What did that even mean?

Kwima lived at the Baptist mission with his mother, sister, and father, who was a pastor. Like me, he was a refugee from Rwanda, but he and his family had moved to Ruanguba several years before. Straightening himself, he walked across the room and sat in a chair that almost touched mine. "You are very sad, Bosco," he observed. "You try to pretend that everything is fine, but I can see it in your eyes that you are not fine." He paused and gave me a questioning look. I said nothing. With an encouraging smile, he concluded, "Jesus Christ is the solution you need. Come, follow me." He abruptly rose to his feet and beckoned to me with his hand. "I want you to meet someone."

Kwima was about a year older than me, and I liked and respected him. The authority with which he spoke, coupled with the accuracy of his observation about my innermost feelings, captured my attention. I was also intrigued by his question. I had never thought about what it might mean to "know Jesus." I sensed that Kwima was asking about something more than simply whether I believed in God. I could easily answer yes to that question. But his question about "knowing Jesus" was different, and I was unsure how to respond. So without saying a word, I gathered my books, and moments later we were walking out of the schoolyard together. My silence during this entire exchange was not surprising. It was widely known at school that, outside of the dance group, I was withdrawn and rarely spoke.

Kwima did not take me to his father as I had thought he might. Instead, he took me to the home of a different Baptist pastor whom I had seen before but had never met. This pastor's daughter was in my class at school, and I had often admired her. She was different from the other students. Always joyful, well-behaved, and smart, she earned high grades in every subject we studied. Kwima introduced me to Pastor Isaiah, who welcomed me warmly into his home. Pastor Isaiah was Kwima's mentor, and it was obvious from the way they greeted each other that they had a good relationship. The three of us chatted casually together for several minutes before Kwima stood and said goodbye.

Suddenly I was alone with Pastor Isaiah. I felt a little awkward because I was still unsure of my reason for being there. But Pastor Isaiah was relaxed and friendly. He offered me a drink and then began to tell me about himself. He was a family man, kind and gentle. He was also Rwandan, but like so many in Ruanguba, he had moved to Zaire years earlier. I felt quite comfortable speaking with him, and so when he started asking me questions, it did not take long for me to open up and begin to share painful details about my past, my family, and all that I had gone through over the past year. When he invited me to come back for another visit in a couple of days, I agreed.

It was probably on my second or third visit to Pastor Isaiah's home that he pulled out a small booklet entitled *The Four Spiritual Laws*.[1] I told him I had never seen the booklet before and did not know what it was about. With that, he reached for his Bible and invited me to join him at a small table, where he placed the Bible next to the open booklet. He then began to speak—slowly, clearly, and softly—as he read alternatively from the booklet and the Bible before adding his own commentary on what he had read. There was a gravity in his tone that conveyed the importance of his message, and I was riveted by his simple yet profound explanation of the four "laws." God loves me and has a plan for my life. My sins have separated me from God. Jesus is the bridge between me and God because he sacrificed his perfect life on the cross to remove the barrier of sin. And finally, by faith, I must receive Jesus as my Savior and Lord in order to fully experience God's love and plan for my life.

Pastor Isaiah read the scriptures that elaborated on the meaning of each "law" to help me understand. This was useful, but it was an illustration that even more effectively penetrated my teenage mind and brought clarity to the moment. A picture panel in the booklet showed a man carrying a heavy load that he then deposited at the foot of the cross. The image of the man laying down his burden helped me to understand what it meant to give my life to Jesus. Pastor Isaiah elaborated. Jesus, he said, could replace my worry with peace and give me direction. If I allowed him. Through prayer, Bible study, and fellowship with other believers, he continued, I could learn to "know Jesus" and it would become easier to obey his word and to relinquish control of my life to him.

My mind was racing. I realized that for the past year I had been carrying an overwhelming load that threatened to crush me. Although the Patrick family had helped and dancing with my friends had provided temporary relief, no one and nothing had succeeded in permanently lifting my load of pain. Even when people had said, "I am praying for you," it had done nothing for me. Other people were laughing and enjoying life, but my life had stopped. I was alive on the outside, but inside I was dead. No one seemed to know that. Or if they did, they didn't know what to do about it. No one, that is, until Kwima and Pastor Isaiah intervened. They recognized that what I needed more than anything else in the world was the "good news" of the Gospel message of love, hope, and forgiveness.

It was almost too much for me to take in at once. I still had so many questions about what truly "knowing Jesus" would mean for me. Nevertheless, something stirred within me as Pastor Isaiah spoke, and when he asked if I wanted to repent of my sins and accept Jesus as my personal Savior, I responded without hesitation: "Yes."

Immediately, it was as if a faucet from which peace flowed through my body had been turned on. The sensation penetrated every fiber of me, and I knew in that very moment that Jesus had come to reside in my heart. While my circumstances had not changed, I had changed.

The next Sunday I went to church for the first time since arriving in Zaire. I recall that I had a small blue New Testament Bible in my pocket. I think Pastor Isaiah must have given it to me. This was my first time in church since the genocide had disrupted my life. The sermon the pastor preached that morning was based on Galatians 5:13–26 which, among other things, contrasts the behavior of those who are guided by the Spirit of God with the behavior of those who are guided by their own will and desires. After he finished speaking, the pastor invited all who wanted to publicly profess their faith in Jesus, repent of their wrongdoing, and begin a new life in relationship with Jesus to stand and walk down the aisle. Realizing my own sinful condition and need to draw closer to Christ, I almost ran to the altar at the front of the church.

I would later compare that moment of revelation to the story of Jesus healing a blind man.[2] In that biblical account, Jesus touched the eyes of the blind man and then asked him, "Can you see anything now?" The man responded, "I see people, but I can't see them very clearly. They look like trees walking around." Jesus then touched the man's eyes a second time. The result? The Bible states his sight was completely restored and he could see everything clearly.

For me, the "first touch" had occurred during my talks with Pastor Isaiah. In church that Sunday morning, I received the "second touch" from Jesus, and it resulted in perfect mental and spiritual clarity regarding what I needed to do—*simply believe.*

CHAPTER 12
A New Beginning

I n the weeks that followed, the Bible became my close companion. I read it in the morning, in the middle of the day, and at night. It seemed I could not ingest enough of it! I was mostly drawn to passages that spoke of the promises of God because the words filled me with so much hope. Not surprisingly, given the sense of loss I felt as a result of being separated from my family, one of my favorite promises was this: "God will never fail you nor abandon you."[1] It was among the first that I committed to memory.

The burden that had begun to lift following my public confession of faith during that memorable Sunday service continued to ease, and I frequently smiled to myself, joyful in the knowledge that my life's journey to become more Christlike in thought and deed had begun. I had prayerfully sought God's forgiveness that morning and told those present that I believed in Jesus, in his power to forgive me, and in his power to bless me with eternal life. The change that was taking place within me was almost tangible.

But I still had a long way to go on my spiritual journey. For example, I was unaware at that time just how strong and deeply rooted in my heart and mind were the destructive emotions of hatred and anger. Fed by everything that had happened to me since April 1994, both had grown and flourished unchallenged inside of me for more than a year in Zaire. Without a doubt, Jesus had begun to transform my way of thinking and feeling. I knew my renewal was well underway. But there was so much I still needed to learn if I was to think like him, speak like him, and act like him. Yes, I knew that Jesus had forgiven me and that he no longer held any of my sins against me. But the big question for me was this: *Would I ever be able to do the same for those who had ruined my life and caused me so much pain?*

Perhaps the most striking and outwardly visible evidence of my new faith was that I became more friendly. Since arriving in Zaire, I had managed to keep most of my classmates at a distance. Although I had interacted with my peers in the dance group and during the occasional soccer game, I rarely smiled and had typically responded to their overtures of friendship in a cold and dismissive manner. Most students soon grew tired of being rebuffed in this way and left me alone to stew in the bitterness of my suffering. But Jesus changed all that almost immediately, and within a few days of my becoming a believer, everyone noticed. But none were more perplexed by my transformation than the members of my dance group.

"I give it a month, Bosco," said Ahadi, one of the best dancers in my group. He had a big grin on his face. "You'll get tired of this Christian thing and return to your old self soon enough." Several of the boys and girls standing around giggled as they nodded their heads in agreement. "Yeah," added Lucien, another member of the group. "You only joined those church people because you can't find your parents and you think they can help you." I was hurt by Lucien's words, but I tried not to show it. I had just told Ahadi, Lucien, and the other students in the dance group that I could no longer be a part of the club.

"I don't understand," said Pascaline. "Dancing is your very favorite thing to do, and you are so good at it! Why would you stop now?" Her brow was furrowed, and she seemed genuinely perplexed.

Looking into the confused faces of my friends, I tried my best to explain that it was not that I believed dancing to be inherently wrong. After all, didn't King David, whom God said was a man after his own heart, dance before the Lord? Rather, it was the *type* of dancing that we performed that was problematic and incompatible with my newfound faith. Zairian popular dance was extremely sensual, and the lyrics of many of the songs to which we danced were sexually suggestive. In contrast, when people in the Bible danced, it was a joyful part of worship—an act of praise to God. "When I dance now," I said, "it will be the kind of dancing that will please God."

My statement was greeted with silence. Several of my peers shook their heads in bewilderment and walked away. But I could tell that a handful were intrigued by what I had said. It was this latter group with whom I would subsequently share my faith and newly acquired biblical knowledge in the days and weeks to come. I was surprised by how very much I enjoyed sharing what I had discovered about Jesus with them. I was beginning to understand what it meant to be "filled with the joy of the Lord."[2]

Unfortunately, opposition to my faith extended beyond the dance group. One night, as I returned home from a prayer meeting with fellow believers at the church, I was greeted by Olive, Mr. Patrick's oldest daughter. She appeared to be angry.

"You cannot come in, Bosco," she shouted. "You have allowed that cult to fill your head with all kinds of nonsense. If you do not promise to reject this foolishness, I will not allow you to stay with us anymore."

I was very hurt. "They are not a cult," I insisted. "They are Baptist pastors and missionaries who believe in Jesus. They teach me what is in the Bible."

I knew that Olive and the entire Patrick family were Christians, so I was surprised by her extreme response. But Olive had grown up attending a church in a different denomination where the services were more formal and scripted and the congregation was quiet and reserved during worship. She did not understand the expressive, exuberant manner with which I now expressed my faith. It made her uncomfortable that the singing and preaching in my new church were louder and more animated than she was used to seeing. To her, the spontaneity and intensity with which we prayed seemed strange, while I, on the other hand, fully embraced the energy and vitality exhibited by my new Christian friends.

That night my pleas to be allowed inside fell on deaf ears as Olive slammed the door in my face. I was shocked and suddenly afraid. Olive had only shown me affection and acceptance over the years, and I could not believe what had just happened. I walked over to a nearby tree and sat on the ground. I could hear the voices of the Patrick children inside, but no one looked out the window or opened the door to check on me. I was sure someone would eventually call me to come inside. But no one did. After sitting and waiting for about an hour, I stretched out on the grass under the tree and closed my eyes. The cool night air penetrated my thin shirt, making it difficult for me to sleep.

The next morning I walked over to Kwima's house and told him what had happened. "I am so sorry, Bosco," he said. "Come with me; I know a place where you can stay." He took me to the home of a young couple who lived not far from the hostel. Habimana and his wife, Sentwali, were also Rwandan missionaries who had settled in Ruanguba several years earlier. They listened sympathetically when Kwima explained my predicament.

"You can stay with us as long as you need to," said Habimana. Sentwali also nodded in agreement. They had two young sons, and I was overcome by their kindness and willingness to share what little space they had with someone whom they had only just met.

Fortunately, I did not have to impose on Habimana and his family for long. About two days after Olive had banished me, Mr. Patrick returned from a trip to Goma. He was upset when he heard what Olive had done and sent his son Jean-Claude to find me and bring me home. Olive apologized, and we never spoke of the incident again.

Later that evening Mr. Patrick pulled me aside and told me the news that I had waited so long to hear. While completing a delivery at a refugee camp near Goma, he had met a fellow businessman who had told him he had information about my parents.

I was so excited I jumped out of my chair.

"What did he tell you? Does he know where they are? When can I meet him?"

As I peppered Mr. Patrick with questions, I failed to notice that he avoided eye contact with me. That should have been my first clue that something was very wrong, but I missed it completely. The second clue I overlooked was Mr. Patrick's evasive response.

"I don't really know much," he said. "But I have a delivery to make at his camp this weekend. You should come along with me. You will be able to meet him and ask him all of your questions. Together we can find out everything he knows about your family."

I could barely sit still during the drive to meet with Fisher, the nickname Mr. Patrick used to refer to his friend in the camp. The camp was four hours away. All I could think about was the fact that after all this time, I had finally found someone who knew my parents and could tell me where they were. But that was not the only good news

Mr. Patrick had delivered. He also told me that he had found Francois! The thought of seeing my friend and protector again brought a wide smile to my face. I remembered the last time I had seen him. He had stood between me and the man who had accused me of being a Tutsi spy moments before I had turned and raced through the forest to safety. I could not wait to thank him for saving my life.

About three hours into our journey, we arrived at the refugee camp where Francois had settled. As he approached the truck, I jumped out and ran to greet him with a hug that lasted a long time. "You look good, Bosco," he said with a smile. "You have grown up a bit, I think."

There was so much I wanted to say, but all I could manage at the moment was a weak whisper. "Yes. I have." With that, we both climbed into the truck, and Mr. Patrick accelerated down the road toward Fisher's camp.

As the lush greenery of the countryside flashed by the windows, the three of us chatted about our experiences over the past two years and reminisced about our lives before April 1994. As happy as we were to be reunited, the mood was bittersweet. After about thirty minutes, my curiosity got the better of me and I tentatively asked Francois what had happened after I ran away that day in the forest. He told me Pierre had shot the man who had wanted to kill me. Our conversation stopped abruptly as Mr. Patrick and I digested the shocking revelation. I decided then that I would not ask whether the man had lived or died. I was too afraid to find out.

Finding Fisher once we arrived at his camp proved to be a challenge. The refugee camp was teeming with people, and tents dotted the landscape as far as the eye could see. I followed behind Mr. Patrick as he walked slowly through the mass of humanity, periodically stopping to make inquiries and converse with individuals along the way. It was almost an hour after we arrived that we heard a shout in the distance. Peering through the throngs of people, I saw a man waving his arms and beckoning to us. Mr. Patrick broke into a smile and ran to meet Fisher.

The two men greeted each other enthusiastically with much laughter and slaps on the back. It was clear they knew each other well. Then Mr. Patrick ushered Francois and me forward and introduced us. Fisher shook our hands before disappearing into his tent and reemerging a few seconds later with two folding chairs, one in each hand. He motioned for Mr. Patrick and me to sit, while both he and Francois remained standing.

As I took a seat on the edge of the chair he offered, my eyes shifted between Fisher and Mr. Patrick. They continued to chat as if this were a purely social visit. I could not tell whether they were intentionally procrastinating or were genuinely oblivious to how eager I was for news of my parents. Finally, Mr. Patrick reminded him of the reason for our visit, and Fisher turned to look directly at me. He cleared his throat and hesitated for several long seconds.

"Your parents and your brothers and sisters moved into the same building where I was living in Gitamara," he said at last. "But then things began to get really bad."

He paused and looked around, as if afraid someone would overhear our conversation. Lowering his voice, he continued. "They were not the only ones. A lot of people from around Kigali came to the area. It was very crowded." He took a deep breath. There were several refugees milling around, but no one seemed at all interested in our small group, which was huddled together in front of the tent. "I told your father that we should leave, escape to the north, but he said he couldn't. He told me, 'Look at my wife. They will kill her and my children.'"

Fisher closed his eyes as he repeated my father's words. When he reopened them, his expression communicated more than the words he spoke. He did not have to say any more. I knew in that instant that my family was dead.

To an onlooker, it may have appeared that Fisher still had my attention, but my thoughts had skittered off to a different time and place. Random scenes from my childhood floated in and out of my mind's eye—scenes that featured each member of my family. Papa, whom I knew loved me more than he could say. Maman, who pampered me and with whom I shared so many treasured moments. Francoise and Marie-Jeanne, my closest friends. Claudine, my rival and occasional ally. Twahirwa and Niyitegeka, my little brothers with whom I wished I could have spent more time. I loved them all so much.

Suddenly Fisher stopped speaking. I looked up and saw that Mr. Patrick and Francois were staring at me. They did not appear to be surprised, and I understood then that they had already known what Fisher was going to say. They had thought it best that I hear the story directly from him. I slowly rose from my chair and, without a word, shook Fisher's hand and walked back to the truck to wait for the others. As I waited, I realized that even as I had become preoccupied with those scenes from my childhood, my ears had captured everything else that Fisher had said.

He had gone on to explain that my father decided he would remain in Gitamara for a few more days before heading south. Apparently, Papa was convinced that Maman and my sisters and brothers would be safer if they relocated to an area where there were larger numbers of Tutsis living. "I said goodbye to your father at that point, and I headed north with many others," Fisher continued. A few days later, he received word of intense fighting in Gitamara and learned that a bomb had leveled the building where my family was staying. "I am sorry," he said. "Everyone was killed."

For two years I had cultivated hope in my heart, and now, in a matter of minutes, that hope was completely gone. I was forced to accept reality. I would never see my family again. Shock can cause people to respond in any number of ways. I think the enormity of the news caused me to just close my eyes and sink into a very deep sleep. So deep was my sleep that I have little memory of our return trip to Ruanguba, except for the brief moment when I awoke to bid farewell to Francois at his camp. I would not see him again for almost seven years.

Prior to learning that my family had been killed, the missionaries and my other friends at church had prayed for their safe return. Now they prayed for Jesus to give me the strength to bear this new burden. I was so thankful that I had not discovered what had happened to my family before I had committed my life to Christ. When I consider the frailty of my emotional condition and mental state prior to embarking on this new relationship with Jesus, I have no doubt that the news would have destroyed me. But now, upheld by faith and by the prayers and support of fellow believers, I experienced a peace that I was incapable of understanding. It filled my innermost being and enabled me to maintain my sanity.

The timing was unbelievable. Jesus allowed me to receive unbearable news only after I had accepted him into my life and asked him to bear every burden on my behalf. I was amazed by this expression of his love, goodness, and grace to me. And this was only the first time. In the months and years to come, Jesus's impeccable timing and his ability to favorably orchestrate pivotal experiences in my life would constantly surprise me.

I will be forever grateful for the members of my church, who became my family. That community of believers in Ruanguba attended to my well-being like true brothers and sisters. They directed me to meditate on scriptures that lifted my spirit and gave me the wisdom I needed to navigate my grief. I also received insights that provided even more reason for me to praise Christ and celebrate all of his promises to me, especially his promise of eternal life. I remembered, for example, how I had grown up in riches but that wealth had vanished almost overnight, like a puff of smoke on a windy day. It confirmed what I had read in scripture about the folly of relying on material possessions rather than on Jesus and his provision.

Similarly, I had assumed my parents would always be around and that I had a secure future working in Papa's business. But that too vanished in a moment. Jesus was now my Father, and unlike my biological father, my new Father would always be there. And although I did not know it at that time, today I can look back and see the great irony. While I had once believed that I would eventually work in my earthly father's business, years later I would receive the call to become a pastor and eventually work in my heavenly Father's "business"—the church. These insights and promises encouraged me immensely back then and continue to do so today.

Yet, as much as my faith and friends helped me to cope in the weeks after I learned that my family had been killed, I still struggled. For years to come, intense rage, unyielding unforgiveness, and overwhelming hatred would join forces to periodically wage battle against the Holy Spirit that was at work within me. I am firmly convinced that had I not actively sought fellowship with my brothers and sisters in Christ and regularly engaged in Bible study, fasting, and prayer, I may very well have succumbed to my own worse instincts and turned my back on Jesus and all that I knew to be true. But thanks be to God, who held me during my darkest moments, the deep pain that fueled my ugly emotions did not win the victory. Not then, nor in the years to come.

As I entered grade nine, in the latter half of 1996, I made another life-changing decision. Mr. Patrick had announced that it was time for the children who were still enrolled in high school in Zaire to return with him to Rwanda. Those who had completed high school were given the option of returning to Rwanda or joining their older siblings in Kenya. By this time the family members who had moved to Goma months before had returned to Rwanda safely, while those who had left for Kenya were settled there. There was no longer a need for any of us to remain in Zaire.

I did not want to go back to Rwanda, however. There was nothing there for me but memories that would tear at my soul. Rwanda had caused me tremendous pain, and although I would not admit it to anyone then, deep in my heart I hated the land of my birth and all of the people who lived there. I believed my anger to be justified. They had destroyed my home, my family, my very way of life. At the time I refused to acknowledge the glaring contradiction. Yes, I had accepted Jesus as my Lord and had committed to living a life pleasing to him. And yes, I understood that he commanded those who follow him to forgive those who wrong us. But I was not ready to forgive. For many years I was able to overlook this internal inconsistency and ignore the battle between belief and practice that raged within me. I succeeded because I was able to convince myself that I would not have to face my own disobedience and hypocrisy if I simply refused to acknowledge these negative emotions.

And so when Mr. Patrick told me of the plan for me to return with the other teenagers and attend school in Ruhengeri, I politely asked him if I could stay in Zaire. Habimana and Sentwali, my missionary friends, had already said that I could move in with them. But Mr. Patrick did not immediately agree. "How will you support yourself here in Zaire?" he asked. "I can give you a little money, but I cannot support you living here indefinitely. You should return and live with us in our home in Ruhengeri, Bosco. You will continue to be part of my family." I expressed my appreciation for his immeasurable kindness to me over the years, then explained that I was just not emotionally ready to return yet. He must have understood my inner turmoil because he finally relented and agreed to let me stay.

Within a matter of days, Olive and Gael took Mr. Patrick's truck and set off for Kenya. The plan was for Gael and his other sons to use the vehicle for deliveries in and around Nairobi and between the city and various refugee camps. In this way, they could begin to contribute to their own financial support. Mr. Patrick left with the other children in another truck for Rwanda. As I waved goodbye to this family that had rescued me and saved my very life, I whispered a prayer of thanksgiving and fervently asked the Lord to bless them.

My life in Zaire after the Patrick family left was pleasant and uneventful for some time. I enjoyed living with Habimana and Sentwali, and I continued to do well in school. I also spent much of my free time in church-related activities and grew in faith and in the knowledge of God's word.

But all was not well in Zaire. Violent skirmishes between ethnic factions who harbored different political goals and economic interests were increasing around the country. Roving bands of armed men had begun to terrorize innocent civilians in many communities. Although I was slow to realize what was happening, I would soon find myself in a situation that was eerily similar to that which I had experienced in Rwanda. History was about to repeat itself, and I would soon be on the run again.

PART FOUR

Unexpected Favor

CHAPTER 13
Into the Dark

I knew something was wrong as soon as I arrived at school that morning. Students were huddled in small groups in the schoolyard, whispering to each other. They were clearly agitated, and many had tears in their eyes. Even the adults seemed to be upset. Rather than ushering students into their classrooms, as they would normally have done at that hour, they moved among the groups of boys and girls, hugging some and patting others gently on the back. Several teachers handed tissues to students who had started to sob audibly, while others stood alone and silent in the corner of the schoolyard, staring vacantly at the trees in the distance. It was clear that teaching was the furthest thing from their minds. I soon found out why. My history teacher and French teacher were dead.

Gathering bits and pieces of information as I moved among my peers and teachers, I was able to pull together an incomplete but disturbing account of the events that had led to this horrible outcome. My beloved teachers had apparently been killed by a band of men who were allies of a group of fighters waging war in the region. I never understood fully how it unfolded, but somehow the two teachers, who lived together on the outskirts of town, had become Ruanguba's first victims in a civil war that now threatened us all.

The killing of these two highly respected and influential individuals sent a shock wave through the community. The terror was palpable. Our collective fear rose to a fever pitch a few nights later when the silence was shattered by the sound of distant gunfire. While several of the adults around me debated the reason for the fighting and its proximity to Ruanguba, my mind swirled with memories of Kigali and flames flickering in the sky on the night I ran away. Anxiety fueled my nausea, and I hugged my knees to my stomach as the sound of battle raged in the distance. The men firing those guns were likely the same men who had killed my teachers, I thought. And they were heading my way. I knew then that the peaceful life I had enjoyed for the past two years in Zaire was coming to an end.

Near midnight only a few days later, Habimana walked into my room and announced, "We must leave now. The shooting is louder than ever—they cannot be far away. Sentwali and the boys are almost ready. Gather your things. Hurry!" I knew the plan. Days before several of the missionaries and pastors had gathered to discuss what they would do if we were forced to leave. Some decided their best option was to return to Rwanda, while others expressed a preference for traveling to distant towns in Zaire that they believed would be safe. Habimana and Sentwali had told me that they had friends in Kenya, so their plan was to flee east and eventually make their way through Uganda, then across the border into Kenya. I asked if I could travel with them, and they agreed. My quickly formulated plan was to eventually reunite with the members of the Patrick family who had settled in Kenya's capital city, Nairobi.

Less than thirty minutes later, we were literally running through the forest in a desperate effort to escape. I could hardly believe it was happening again. Once more I was being chased by people I did not know, for reasons I did not understand. The light from the moon revealed hundreds of fellow travelers around us. If I had to guess, I would say that close to one thousand people fled Ruanguba with us that night, all heading toward Uganda. As a group, we moved in fits and starts, alternating between running for a few minutes, then slowing to a quick walk as we attempted to catch our breath. Parents carried infants on their backs and in their arms as older children struggled to keep up. Nearly everyone had packed way too much, and the strain of trying to move swiftly while also carrying heavy loads was visible in the bent bodies and sweat-drenched faces that glistened in the moonlight. Over time the path before us became strewn with belongings as more and more people made difficult decisions to sacrifice food, clothing, and other possessions in favor of maintaining their speed. No one knew for sure if we were being actively pursued and if so, the distance between us and the men who might kill us. We only knew we had to keep moving quickly.

I am not sure how many hours we were on the move, but suddenly there was an opening in the trees. Looming ahead of us was a large farmhouse. It was completely dark. As we slowly walked across the open field toward the house, it became evident that the property had been recently vacated. Potatoes, ripe for harvesting, were strewn across the ground. Scores of people rushed forward to gather the abandoned crop.

"Listen, the shooting has stopped," observed Habimana. "I think it may be safe to rest here for a few hours." Then, glancing back at his young sons, he added, "I don't think the children can walk any farther tonight." I had not heard gunfire or explosions for at least an hour, maybe two. Others seemed to have made that calculation as well because, within minutes, hundreds of people slowly began to sit down in the grass. Sentwali handed me a thin polyethylene blanket. I appreciated the covering and was touched that in the chaos she had thought to pack it for me before leaving the house.

Several hours later I awoke to the sensation of wetness on my face.

As I sat up, I realized that not only was my face damp, but my hair was as well. My breath had condensed on the inside of the strange, crinkly, foil-like blanket and formed droplets that produced the cold dampness that had interrupted my sleep. I glanced around the field and could see that others had also begun to stir. All traces of drowsiness were erased when I realized just how vulnerable we were in our current location. Hundreds of unarmed men, women, and children, sleeping in an open field. We were entirely visible to anyone who might emerge from the trees that surrounded us. And the sun was already rising. It was definitely time to go.

There was no running now, just a steady and determined pace as we marched together to the Ugandan border. Along the way, we consumed all of the remaining food we had packed. When hunger returned, we resorted to pulling up wild roots and eating them raw. I recall that they were surprisingly sweet, no doubt made more palatable by the pain of hunger.

My situation was all too familiar. I had never imagined that I would experience this once in my life, much less twice. I had grown up in a large, beautiful home that was filled with abundance and love, so how could this now be my reality? Yet it was. At the age of seventeen, I was hungry, afraid, and dirty, with no house, family, or even country to call my own. My newfound faith gave me a boldness, however, that I had not had before. As I walked along, I silently called out to Jesus and demanded an answer: *When will my suffering end?* Discerning no immediate response, I resolved to pray unceasingly until he answered. I also decided to cling faithfully to the promise that permeates scripture: Jesus will never abandon us regardless of how grim our circumstances might appear.

A few hours later, Habimana, who had been walking a short

distance behind me, drew alongside and alerted me to a problem that had not even crossed my mind. "The Ugandan authorities will not allow you to cross the border with only your school identification card," he observed. He was right. I had no travel documents. Worse, I was from Rwanda, not Zaire, which would further complicate my immigration status. "What should I do?" I asked Habimana. He did not answer right away. In the silence I began to worry. *What will happen to me if the Ugandans deny me entry to their country? Where will I go? And what about the gang of men chasing us? They will surely catch up to me and kill me on sight.* I felt so helpless.

Then Habimana spoke: "I have Zairian travel documents that will allow me and my family to cross the border. Everyone's name is listed in the document, but there is space enough to add another name. This is what I will do. I will write in your name. They will think you are my oldest son."

I was speechless. Habimana and Sentwali were willing to risk everything—their future and the future of their children—for me. If the forgery was discovered, who knew what the Ugandan authorities would do to them and to me? What had I done to merit such favor from a young couple who barely knew me? Later, as I marveled at the mercy and grace of Jesus toward me, that moment would stand out as a shining example of heavenly intervention into my circumstances. "Thank you," I whispered.

After many more hours of walking, we finally approached the Ugandan border. I was filled with trepidation. From the corner of my eye, I noticed that Habimana's hand shook nervously as he handed the uniformed border official the documents. The official eyed us with suspicion, barely disguising his disgust. We were filthy, smelly, and exhausted. I can only imagine that, to him, we must have looked less than human. I held my breath as he reviewed the documents, unwilling to draw any unnecessary attention to my rigid body. Finally, he handed the documents back to Habimana, nodded, and waved us through. Now I struggled not to leap in the air for joy! I had made it safely into Uganda.

But my elation evaporated almost immediately after crossing the border. We were met by Ugandan soldiers and ushered to a nearby refugee camp. We soon learned that we were not authorized to travel through the country to Kenya or to anywhere else in Uganda. We had not expected that our freedom would be so severely restricted. Our plan to continue on to Kenya would have to be put on hold for the time being.

The camp to which we were taken was makeshift and temporary. We were informed that plans were underway to move all twenty thousand refugees in the camp to a permanent site in the near future. For now, however, this camp would be our home. Officials from the United Nations were in charge of operations, and upon our arrival, they handed us blankets, utensils, and materials to build our own shelter. They explained that we would have to go to the forest on the outskirts of the camp to cut the wood necessary to frame our tents. "You will need to collect firewood from the forest, too, so you can cook your food," added a member of the UN team as he handed Habimana a small axe. While we were forbidden to leave the area around the camp, we were allowed to go into the small town just outside of the camp in order to purchase personal items. But no further. The refugee camp, I concluded, was little more than a prison. My dream of reaching Nairobi seemed far out of reach.

Habimana and Sentwali were given supplies for themselves and their children, but I was considered to be an adult single male and treated differently. I was provided my own bedding and tent-making materials and was told I would have to share my tent with another adult male. "You will share your tent with him," the UN representative said, gesturing toward a young man who had been standing quietly nearby. Like nearly all of the other refugees, he was from Zaire, and I guessed his age to be around twenty-five years old. He introduced himself to us as Robert, and with a smile, he reached over to help gather up the utensils and blankets that had been distributed to us. The two of us followed Habimana, Sentwali, and the children to a clearing where we laid our belongings down in the grass. With Robert's help, we were able to build both our tents and store our belongings in a relatively short period of time.

The camp was a sprawling mass of humanity as far as the eye could see. Memories of the camps in and around Goma that I had visited while searching for my parents came to mind. I had never imagined that one day I would be forced to live in a place like this. The air was thick with smoke that swirled among the tents and permeated the fabric of our clothes. Early in the morning people would rise and start small fires in front of their tents to cook breakfast. These fires would burn all day, whether or not the family inside was actually cooking a meal. The nearby forest was thick with trees, so there was no shortage of wood to burn. Everything and everyone smelled like smoke, which would cause our eyes to water and our nostrils to sting. The incessant smoke was like a blanket that permanently covered the camp. It was impossible to get away from it.

Life in the camp was slow-paced. Our routine consisted of gathering firewood, cooking, and little else. A few individuals in the camp had radios, and we would try to get close enough to one of them during news reports in the evenings. It was difficult to hear because of the crowds that would congregate to listen. Sometimes I would just sit back and watch the young children run around and play instead. They appeared to be so happy, without a care in the world. They had no idea what was happening. I envied their lack of awareness and ability to find joy in these barren surroundings. Invariably, I would begin to cry. Not so long ago, my own carefree childhood had been suddenly and brutally snatched away. Now I carried the weight of my memories and dreams of a future that was terrifyingly uncertain.

Robert was easygoing and likable, and it did not take long for us to become friends. He shared little about his background or how he came to be alone in the camp, and I did not pry. Our conversations centered on the present moment and where we might go from here. Habimana and Sentwali welcomed Robert as well. Although he and I slept in a separate tent next to theirs, we combined all our food rations and ate our meals together in Habimana's tent. To the casual onlooker, we appeared to be members of a single family.

Although life in the camp was not ideal, I gave thanks to God for what I had. The UN provided us rations that included beans, maize, powdered milk, biscuits, and cooking oil. We would line up to receive our rations on a particular day each week, so we always had enough to eat. On a different day, the camp distributed water for cooking, drinking, and washing ourselves. We were also pleasantly surprised to discover a small group of Christians in the camp who held periodic worship meetings. We participated enthusiastically in these gatherings, which refreshed our spirits and helped relieve the monotony of camp life. Together with my daily Bible reading and prayer time, I continued to be spiritually sustained during my time in the camp.

Although I was grateful that I had escaped from Zaire and that I had food, shelter, and companionship, I knew I could not continue in this state of suspension indefinitely. I had nothing meaningful to do and nothing to occupy my mind besides reading the scriptures. After the first few weeks, I began to grow restless. When the boredom became unbearable, I would join Habimana or Robert for a slow walk into town, not because I needed to buy anything but simply for a change of scenery.

The Rwandan border was not far from the camp. This made me somewhat nervous because I had heard that refugees from Zaire could stay in Uganda but the authorities were forcing Rwandans to go back home. I decided to keep a low profile, to stick close to Habimana or Robert at all times, and to say as little as possible. While we all conversed in French, Habimana, Sentwali, and Robert each spoke with a distinctive Zairian accent that I had not acquired. I still spoke French like a Rwandan, and I feared that my accent might reveal my nationality and put me at risk for deportation.

Not surprisingly, I was beyond excited when I learned that Habimana and Sentwali had begun to plan our escape from the camp. One evening, as we ate dinner, Habimana mentioned he had heard that our temporary camp was to be closed very soon, perhaps in a couple of weeks. At this point we had already been living in Uganda for two months. "If they move us to the other camp, it will be more difficult for us to make our way to Kampala," Habimana explained. "Security will be tighter. More soldiers, I'm sure."

Habimana had told me weeks earlier that he had a friend who was the pastor of a church in Uganda's capital city, Kampala. This pastor had promised to help us get to Kenya if we could make it to his house in the city. "We must leave soon," Habimana continued earnestly. "Or it could be a very long time before we have another opportunity." Habimana, Sentwali, and I spoke freely in front of Robert, who had previously revealed to us that he, too, wanted to get to Kenya. We had already decided that any secret plan to escape would have to include our new friend. "When are we leaving?" he asked. I could tell he was as excited as I was.

Over the course of the next week, we figured out the details. Sentwali had discovered there was a bus that left early every morning bound for Kampala. The challenge for us was to figure out how to leave the camp and board the bus without arousing suspicion. Bus drivers and even some locals were known to have alerted the authorities when they spotted individuals whom they suspected of being refugees trying to leave the camp. Since arriving, we had heard rumors of several refugees being caught and returned to camp after attempting to board one of these buses. It was therefore imperative that we blend in with everyone else who would be boarding the bus.

This was easier said than done. Our bodies, our clothes, and our shoes were dirty most of the time, and our hair was often disheveled and full of dust. Like all the other refugees, we looked a mess. We knew that we would not be able to leave if we could not improve our appearance, so we set out to do just that in the days leading up to our escape.

First, we identified the very best items of clothing we each possessed and washed them with extra care and attention. We scrubbed every inch of fabric over and over again before carefully laying them in the sun to dry. Our shoes received similar attention. Using water and old rags, we rubbed off as much dust and dirt as we could before setting them aside for that special morning. The evening before our planned departure, we bathed our bodies with the limited water and soap available. We focused especially on our face, hair, hands, and fingernails—everywhere that would be visible and where accumulated dust and dirt might suggest we were anything other than the typical Ugandan family we were pretending to be.

That night Robert and I were too excited to sleep more than a couple of hours. Our few belongings were stacked carefully in the far corner of the tent. Next to us were our clean clothes, shoes, and two small bags. My bag was barely big enough to accommodate the extra pants and shirt I had stuffed inside next to my Bible, a pen, my school identification card, and a small notebook. Those were the only items I would be taking with me in the morning. Robert's bag was similarly stuffed with what he considered essential. Habimana and Sentwali had warned us that if we left the camp with more than a single small bag, it might reveal that we had no intention of returning.

"I won't miss any of those things," I whispered to Robert, glancing at the utensils, blankets, and tools stacked in the corner. "I just want to leave this place."

"Yes," agreed Robert. "Whoever wants them after we leave is welcome to have them. I don't care."

We did not all leave the camp at the same time the next morning. Four adults and two children marching out together would have attracted too much attention. Sentwali and the two boys left first, followed by Habimana and me about fifteen minutes later. We told Robert to wait another ten minutes before following us. It was still quite early, and only a few people were milling around as we walked between the tents toward the road that led to town. A couple of people glanced at us as we walked by, but most were preoccupied with crying babies or with getting their fire started for the day. Habimana and I walked confidently toward the bus stop, where Sentwali and the children were standing with a handful of people who were also waiting. Before leaving their tent, Sentwali had warned the boys to be silent. They didn't fully understand what was happening, but they smiled without saying a word when they saw their father and me approaching. Here, in the middle of all these Ugandans, speaking French would have immediately revealed that we were foreigners and likely refugees. We had to remain silent for our plan to work.

I casually glanced around at the other passengers to see how our group compared. While most wore nicer clothes than we did, our clothes were presentable. I was so glad we had taken the extra time to clean up. There was little difference between our fellow passengers and us, and in the dim early-morning light, we blended in fairly well.

Just then the bus pulled up, and I turned around to see Robert walking hurriedly toward us. As we all boarded the bus, Habimana handed the driver a few American dollars that he had brought with him from Zaire, to cover our fare. Paying for goods and services with American currency was fairly common. Residents of many border towns, who often moved from one country to another to visit relatives or conduct business, often used American currency rather than their own national currency, which was of no value once they crossed any of the international borders. Had we displayed Zairean currency, it would definitely have raised the bus driver's suspicion, in addition to the currency being worthless. Later, when I realized how easily we might have inadvertently revealed our identity as Zairean refugees, I breathed a sigh of relief. Habimana and Sentwali had planned ahead and had come prepared with American money, while I had given no thought to such matters. And so, as I had done on so many prior occasions, I thanked God for this couple and for paving the way to my friendship with them.

We headed to the back of the bus, where there were still several open seats. We hoped to avoid the prying eyes of the driver, our traveling companions, and any Ugandan military officials who might be passing by. About five minutes after everyone settled into their seats, the driver pressed the horn loudly, paused for a few seconds, then closed the bus door. As the bus slowly pulled away from the curb, we looked at each other and exhaled. We had made it.

CHAPTER 14

The Crossing

Sweet bananas! One of the things that I remember most about that bus ride from the refugee camp to the city of Kampala was eating a lot of bananas. Along the way we stopped several times to allow passengers to get on and off, and at each of these stops, we purchased the most delicious bananas I had ever tasted in my life. While Uganda is perhaps best known for its high-quality coffee, I can attest that its bananas are similarly excellent.

I also recall that the journey seemed to take forever—at least twelve hours, I think. Although we had ample opportunities to purchase food, stretch our limbs, and relieve ourselves discreetly in wooded areas not far from the road, I became more and more restless as time dragged on. By the time the sun was beginning to set, I wanted to get off the bus for good.

It was dark when our bus finally pulled up at the bus stop in Kampala. As we disembarked, I was surprised to see a middle-aged man emerge from the shadows and rush toward Habimana. The two men embraced warmly. The man then turned and said a quick hello to each of us before ushering us toward his car, which was parked across the street. It was not a very spacious vehicle, but we managed to squeeze in ourselves and our belongings, close the doors, and drive off quickly into the night.

I learned that Habimana's friend was a pastor and that they had worked together years before as missionaries. I have no idea how he knew to meet us at the bus stop at that precise time, but I didn't ask any questions. I figured that somehow, in the days prior to our departure from the refugee camp, Habimana must have gotten word to him regarding our travel plans. Habimana was resourceful, so I was not surprised that he was able to execute a plan like this despite the limitations in our ability to communicate.

The pastor drove us to a small guesthouse that was next door to his church. Although he welcomed us warmly, it was evident that he was nervous. He had driven quickly through the city and kept looking over his shoulder as we walked from the car to the front door of the guesthouse. As we each took a seat in the small kitchen, he explained why he was so fearful. If he were to be caught by the Ugandan police giving aid to refugees who had illegally left a refugee camp, he would be severely punished. For that reason, he did not want his neighbors or his family, who were in one of the houses close by, to see us. He then gave us strict instructions to stay indoors with the windows closed. We were tired and afraid and had no intention of disobeying his wishes.

Later that night I experienced three things that made that night in Kampala memorable. First, the pastor provided us with a delicious dinner that he brought over from his house. I do not remember what he gave us to eat, but it was the first meal I had consumed in recent memory that was served in a real house, around a dining table, and with proper cutlery and plates. Next, he gave us towels and showed us to the bathroom, where we were each able to take a hot shower. After months of washing up in cold water from a small plastic bucket, the scent of sweet soap and the feel of warm water flowing over my entire body from head to toe felt like extreme luxury. When the pastor showed me to a bedroom and I slid between the sheets on a bed with a soft mattress, I thought I was dreaming. It was incredible.

The next morning I rose early and put on the same clothes I had worn the day before. I still had the extra shirt and pants in my bag, but I wanted to save that outfit for another time since it was unclear when next I would be able to wash my clothes. But it didn't matter. I was still energized and happy from being treated so unexpectedly well the night before. Yes, my clothes were worn and a little soiled, but I felt hopeful.

I entered the kitchen to find Habimana and Sentwali engaged in deep conversation with our host. "Come, eat some breakfast," said the pastor as he waved me toward an empty chair. "Where is your friend?"

I told him that Robert was just waking up. "But he will be ready soon," I assured him. "Good," he responded as he busied himself preparing a plate of food for me. "The bus to Kenya will be departing in a couple of hours, and you don't want to miss it." I was a little disappointed that we would be leaving Kampala so soon. I was not looking forward to getting on a bus again after yesterday's long drive. The thought of spending another night in the pastor's comfortable guesthouse was also very appealing. But I knew that every minute that we were here put our host at risk of being arrested and possibly jailed. We had to keep moving.

As I ate my breakfast, I listened closely to the conversation around me and soon learned that the pastor's generosity extended even further than I could have hoped. He promised to give each of us cash to cover our bus fare and food for the journey, as well as enough money to purchase visas at the Kenyan border, which would allow us to enter the country. The pastor's kindness to Habimana and Sentwali I understood. They were his friends. But why would he treat Robert and me so well? Later, as I grew in my new faith, I would come to understand that the pastor had simply done as Jesus had commanded. He had demonstrated unconditional love to us in the way we needed it most.

Suddenly the pastor turned to me. "So, Bosco, what are you planning to do when you arrive in Kenya, young man?" I told him about the Patrick family and my plan to live with them. "That is good," he said, nodding slowly. "Do you have their address or their telephone number?" I was caught off guard by the question. Up until that point, I had given little thought to exactly how I would find them. I answered nervously but truthfully, "No, sir." The pastor's eyes widened as he turned to look at Habimana and Sentwali, who shrugged in response to his unspoken question. He then returned his gaze to me. "Then how do you plan to locate them?" he asked, genuinely perplexed.

"They are in a place called Nairobi West," I said, trying my best to sound confident. "I will look for them there." As I spoke, I saw the pastor's expression change from surprise to sympathy.

"Bosco, I don't think you understand," he said. "Listen to me." He leaned forward and stared at me intently. "Nairobi is a large and busy city. About two million people live there. You will not be able to find your friends unless you know exactly where you are going. Also, the streets are dangerous. You might get hurt if you have to sleep outdoors." He paused before continuing. "And if the Kenyan police find you roaming the streets without an address or proper travel documents, they will arrest you and throw you in prison. Who knows what will happen to you in there, or when you will be released."

Robert entered the kitchen in time to hear the pastor's dire warnings. His worried expression revealed that he understood fully that what could happen to me in Nairobi could also happen to him.

Like me, Robert had made no concrete plans and had no idea where to go once he arrived in the city. We had understood for some time that we would not be able to live with Habimana and Sentwali in Kenya. They were going to live with a fellow missionary family who had graciously agreed to take them and their two boys into their home. Robert and I knew that invitation did not extend to us. But as unbelievable as it may sound, up until that moment in the kitchen, neither Robert nor I had given much thought to what we would do after arriving in Nairobi. We had been so preoccupied with just getting *to* Nairobi. Now the precariousness of our situation was beginning to dawn on us as we absorbed the pastor's words and noticed the anxious expressions on the faces of Sentwali and Habimana.

Suddenly the pastor's body language changed. He stood up and began to pace around the kitchen, adopting a take-charge attitude. With an air of authority, he sketched out a new plan for Robert and me. "This is what you will do," he said. "Once you arrive in Kenya, do not go directly to Nairobi," he said. "It's way too dangerous in the city. Instead, head north to the Kakuma Refugee Camp. The United Nations office that is located there will be able to help you. They may even be able to locate that family you plan to live with in Nairobi. That is the best you can do for now. At least you will be safe there."

Habimana and Sentwali nodded silently. Even Robert seemed to be persuaded that it was our best option. I did not know what to think at first. I had dreamed about going to Nairobi for so long that the idea of changing my plans at this late stage was hard to accept. It also did not help that the pastor was directing me to go to a refugee camp. I had seen enough of refugee camps in Zaire and Uganda. But what choice did I have? I had no money, no travel documents, and no idea how to get to the only people I knew in Nairobi. And I could not risk being apprehended by the Kenyan authorities. The pastor was probably right, I reasoned. The UN might indeed help me find the Patrick family. After a few moments of tense silence, I looked at the pastor and exhaled slowly. "All right," I said. "That is what we will do."

The pastor drove us to the bus stop about a half hour later, and after thanking him profusely for his kindness, we boarded the bus that would take us to the border. As the bus pulled away, it occurred to me that our arrival in Kampala late the evening before was in some ways like Joseph and Mary arriving in Bethlehem. Mary did not know where she was going to stay in Bethlehem, and I had not known where we were going to stay in Kampala. But unexpectedly, the pastor had appeared and provided a comfortable guesthouse, next to a church, in which we could rest after our long journey. The innkeeper had similarly provided Joseph and Mary a stable in which to rest that was warm and comfortable. I do not remember the exact date, but I do know that it was in December 1996, probably close to Christmas Day, when we left Kampala on the bus ride to Kenya. It was not surprising, therefore, that Mary and Joseph would have been on my mind during that season. While this was unlike any Christmas I had ever experienced before, the thought of my situation being comparable to theirs made me smile.

The bus we boarded in Kampala was luxurious compared to the one we had traveled on the day before. We were clean and well-fed, and our mood was light, almost carefree. The disappointment I had felt about not being able to go directly to Nairobi had lifted, and I chatted happily with my traveling companions.

We arrived at the Kenyan border late in the afternoon. We got off the bus and joined a long line of people who were preparing to cross the border. I could feel my anxiety beginning to rise as we got closer to the building in which the customs officials processed each person seeking entry. I was on my own this time, with no travel documents. Habimana had already explained that he could not alter the documents needed for entry to Kenya as he had done when crossing into Uganda. But I did have a plan. I was going to pretend that I was Ugandan and that I had misplaced my documents. Someone had told us that Ugandans did not need a visa to enter Kenya. I figured that it might be easier for me to be granted entry if the authorities believed me to be a Ugandan teenager who had simply lost his papers rather than a Rwandan refugee. I now realize I was very naïve to think that such an ill-conceived plan would work. But it was all I could think of at the time. Even Habimana was out of good ideas and had offered no alternative solutions to my dilemma.

Robert, Habimana, Sentwali, and their sons were all ahead of me in the line. I had decided to hold back to see how things worked out for them before I approached the officials. I do not know what documents they had as citizens of Zaire, but whatever they handed to the officials was approved. After they purchased their visas, the officials stamped their documents, and I watched through a chain-link fence as they emerged from the small building on the Kenyan side of the border. They turned to smile and wave at me, signaling that all had gone well for them. A few minutes later, it was my turn.

I had not expected to be rejected so quickly. The official who questioned me was interested in only one thing: my travel documents. I tried to explain that I had lost them, but it was clear that he did not believe me. I spoke Swahili with a foreign accent, which no doubt revealed that I was not Ugandan. That fact, coupled with my inability to answer his final question, sealed my fate. "Why are you going to Kenya?" he asked. I opened my mouth to speak, but my brain could not quickly formulate a reasonable response. I just stood there, mouth agape, for several seconds. With that, the Kenyan official waved his hand in irritation and instructed me to turn around and go back to Uganda. I was devastated.

As I walked back toward the area where we had left the bus, I could see my companions on the other side of the fence, waiting. They could see me too. It was obvious what had happened to me, and the concern on their faces was evident even from a distance. They were standing next to a parked bus, which I presumed was the one that would take them to Kisumu and then on to Nairobi. My legs suddenly became weak as I realized that they would be boarding at any moment. Once that bus left, I would be completely alone. I crouched down and sat on the edge of the curb.

I do not know how long we stared at each other through that fence, but eventually my tears blinded me, and I hung my head between my knees. I watched as my tears splattered in the dirt between my shoes. Words cannot adequately describe the feelings I had at that moment. The memory of everything that had happened to me—the pain, terror, and rage I had experienced since 1994—raced through my mind, starting with the moment gangs invaded my home and threatened to kill my dear mother, up to this moment when my hopes and dreams were completely dashed by a customs official at the Uganda-Kenya border. I had an overpowering impulse to scream, loudly and for an extended period of time.

I was on the verge of doing just that when a voice pierced my consciousness. "Are you Bosco?"

I looked up to find a man wearing a customs officer's uniform standing in front of me. "Yes," I responded weakly.

"Good," the man said. "Come with me. Now." He abruptly turned and started walking very quickly toward the small office that I had just left. I hesitated a few seconds before I jumped to my feet, grabbed my small bag, which was resting in the dirt, and ran after him. He strode through the building with assurance, his shoulders back and chin held high. As we approached one of the customs officials responsible for processing travelers, the stranger gestured toward me and said simply, "He is with me." With that, we walked past the desk and continued through the building. As we exited into the sunlight, my companion pointed toward Habimana and Robert, who were still standing beside the bus. They wore huge smiles. "Go," he commanded abruptly. "Your bus to Kisumu will be leaving soon." Before I could even say a word to him, he turned and strode back into the building. And just like that, I achieved my dream. I was in Kenya.

Over the years I have often wondered what exactly happened that day. When I passed through the building and stepped onto Kenyan soil for the first time, I was so shocked I had assumed that I must have fallen asleep and was now dreaming. My situation had evolved so suddenly—from failure to success in the blink of an eye, with no effort whatsoever on my part. How could that be? That customs official must have been an angel, I thought. Or had Habimana bribed him to escort me in? Maybe the customs official had just felt sorry for me and had relented after speaking with Habimana and learning that I was a teenager all alone in a country where I did not even speak the language. There were several possible explanations, but when I asked Habimana what had happened, his only response was to laugh and say, "Let's get a cold soda before the bus leaves. I am sure you have not had one in a long time." I wish now that I had pressed for an answer, but I have resigned myself to the fact that I will never know for sure.

"Sentwali and the boys are already on the bus," explained Habimana as he hurried toward the nearby shops. "It will be several hours before we get to Kisumu, so we should buy some food for the journey." Robert and I followed closely behind him, doing our best to keep up as we stared at the busy scene around us. Buses and smaller vans competed for space on the narrow roadway, even as pedestrians and bicyclists wove in and out of the traffic. Dozens of vendors, who were selling everything from fruit to hot food, lined the sidewalks. They called out to us enthusiastically as we walked by. I rather enjoyed the hustle and bustle of this small border town and wished we could have lingered a little longer.

About fifteen minutes later, we returned to the bus with several small bags full of food and drink and settled into our seats. Eventually the bus driver pressed the horn long and hard, the door closed, and we were on our way. As I sipped my cold soda and gazed out on the Kenyan countryside, which glowed in the orange light of the setting sun, I reflected on the day's events. I was still struggling to digest the astounding fact that I had made it from Zaire to Kenya with nothing but my school identification card, which no one had even bothered to examine.

There is a popular chorus sung in many churches around the world, and it goes like this: "Count your blessings, count them one by one, and you will be surprised to see what the Lord has done." As I put my head back and closed my eyes, I started to count my blessings, which were really miracles. I thought about when the vehicle I was in was attacked with grenades and bullets as I drove from Kigali to Gitamara and yet my life was spared. And when my companions intervened to prevent the Interahamwe from shooting me at point-blank range on two separate occasions, first at the roadblock and days later in the forest. I also recalled how I had arrived at the Patricks' home within two days of them leaving Rwanda for Zaire. Had I reached it after they had departed Ruhengeri, what might have become of me? I had no money or food at the time, so I would likely have ended up in a disease-infested refugee camp in Zaire, all by myself. I shudder even now when I think about how many of my fellow Rwandan countrymen died in the squalor of the camps, even after the genocide ended.

Jesus's perfect timing was also evident later on, when I decided to become his disciple. I may very well have taken my own life had I received the dreadful news that my family had been killed before I had undergone the profound spiritual transformation that occurred when Jesus entered my life. By the time the terrible news was delivered, I was already filled with the Holy Spirit and surrounded by a family of believers who prayed for me constantly. I had also become an avid reader of the Bible, which provided the wisdom and insights that allowed me to cope.

And then there were Habimana and Sentwali. Living and traveling with them, I had witnessed firsthand Jesus's provision and his ability to clear every seemingly insurmountable obstacle out of the way. Their God-guided decision to welcome me into their family had caused my faith to grow by leaps and bounds and changed the entire trajectory of my life. I would never have made it to Kenya without them. Now, as the bus rocked and swayed on its way to Kisumu, I drifted off to sleep. Little did I know that although storms still lay ahead, God's work was not finished. Even more miraculous blessings were on the way.

CHAPTER 15
Angel along the Way

It was close to midnight when we finally arrived in Kisumu. The streets were empty and dark. One single cafe still had its lights on. When the bus driver announced that he would be stopping for a few minutes, several passengers disembarked and followed him into the little establishment. With a quick glance to confirm that their children were fast asleep, Habimana and Sentwali quietly stepped off the bus with Robert and me to stretch their legs. And to say goodbye.

As I stared at Habimana and Sentwali in the dark, a wave of intense sadness washed over me. They had been my family, protecting and providing for me for so many months. I did not know what to say. As I struggled to find the words, Sentwali shook her head and pulled me into a warm embrace. "Shhh, there is no need to say anything," she whispered. I then turned to hug Habimana. He smiled, and I was reminded at that moment that even if we were never to meet again here on earth, we would one day enjoy a heavenly reunion. They would always remain my brother and sister in Jesus Christ.

I have not seen or spoken with Sentwali or Habimana since we parted that night. We had no phone numbers or addresses to exchange, so there was no means of reestablishing contact in the future. They anticipated staying only a short time with the missionary family in Nairobi and had no idea where they would be going next. I was heading to a refugee camp on the other side of the country and had no concrete plans beyond that. There was an air of finality when we hugged that night. I think we all instinctively knew this was the end of a remarkable friendship.

Soon the driver returned to the bus. Habimana shook my hand one last time before turning to join Sentwali and the other passengers who were climbing back on board. When he reached his seat, he saluted me through the open window. I continued to wave until the rear lights on their bus were finally consumed by the darkness.

Our northbound bus was not scheduled to leave Kisumu for another six or seven hours. Robert and I could not afford to rent a room. What little money we had was already earmarked for bus fare and food. We anticipated a most uncomfortable night ahead. "Come, Bosco," said Robert, pointing to the café. "Let's get some tea." He knew I was disheartened, and I could tell he wanted to lift my spirits. I followed him across the street, and we took a seat at a small table near the entrance to the cafe. We sipped our tea in silence.

I already missed my friends terribly. We had gone through so much together, and I was once again experiencing the loneliness that had settled over me when I was running through the forest in Rwanda. Loss had become a recurring theme in my life, and I did not like it at all. Robert's companionship, though I greatly appreciated it, did little to relieve my anguish.

When we emerged from the café about twenty minutes later, we noticed that the temperature had dropped. I reached in my bag for my extra shirt and slipped it on. But even two shirts did little to ward off the chill in the air. We would have liked to have stayed in the café until morning, but the owner had made it clear that it was time for him to lock up for the night, so we walked over to the bus depot and took a seat on the ground outside the office. Within an hour our bodies were stretched out completely. Somehow, we managed to fall asleep on the cold, hard surface.

I will be forever grateful that I did not know the geography of Kenya at that time. If I had been aware of the travel times, road conditions, and distances involved in reaching Kakuma, I would likely have made a very rash decision in Kisumu that night. I would have ignored the pastor's warning and remained on the bus to Nairobi. Fortunately for me, I did not know that Nairobi is only about 350 kilometers from Kisumu, while Kakuma is almost 600 kilometers away. In the opposite direction. As Habimana, Sentwali, and their sons reached Nairobi early the following morning, Robert and I were just waking up to begin our slow, exhausting two-day journey to the refugee camp in the far northwest of the country.

My ignorance of Kenya's landscape protected me from making a huge mistake. As a result, I learned yet another valuable lesson: Jesus's ways of solving problems and resolving difficult situations are always superior to my very best ideas, even when his approach initially appears to be illogical or strange. Weeks later I would remember this moment, and it would confirm for me the wisdom inherent in King Solomon's words: "Trust in the Lord with all your heart; do not depend on your own understanding. Seek his will in all you do, and he will tell you which path to take."[1] It took a major detour to teach me this important lesson, but I have never forgotten that truth.

Our bus arrived shortly after 6:00 a.m. the following morning. Robert and I awoke about an hour before and went to buy tea and bread for our breakfast before getting on board. A quick conversation with the driver revealed that we would be heading to the town of Kitale. There we would switch to a van that would take us to a place called Lodwar. "You will have to spend the night in Lodwar," he added. "The van to the refugee camp in Kakuma won't leave Lodwar till tomorrow morning." I could not hide my disappointment. The thought of spending yet another night outside in a strange town was most unappealing.

We arrived in Kitale in the afternoon. After purchasing something to eat, we boarded the van that would take us to Lodwar. As we settled into our seats, a young woman who appeared to be in her twenties climbed in and took the seat next to me. Our eyes met briefly, and I nodded hello. She responded with a smile. Soon the driver pulled away from the bus stop and began what would turn out to be an almost-eight-hour drive to Lodwar.

There is a scripture that states, "Don't forget to show hospitality to strangers, for some who have done this have entertained angels without realizing it!"[2] God turned the tables on Robert and me on that trip to Lodwar. While we entertained no one, without realizing it, we were on our way to being shown extreme and unexpected hospitality by an angel.

I can no longer remember her name. In fact, I can barely recall what her face looked like. But, for the purpose of this story, I will call her Malaika, which is the Swahili word for "angel." Malaika was the young lady who sat next to me in the van just before we left Kitale for Lodwar. We did not communicate at all for the first hour or two of the journey, but eventually we started to speak to each other haltingly.

Malaika spoke English and a Kenyan version of Swahili, while Robert and I spoke to each other in French and in a Zairian version of Swahili. Neither Robert nor Malaika spoke my native language, Kinyarwanda. Though they are similar, the Swahili spoken in Kenya is different from the Swahili that I had learned in Zaire. So while the three of us were able to communicate using very simple sentences and hand gestures, the language barrier prevented more than superficial conversations.

At one point during the journey, we told Malaika that we were on our way to Kakuma. She was surprised. "That is far away," she said. "You will not be able to go there till tomorrow." A few minutes later, she asked, "Where will you stay when we get to Lodwar? It will be night by the time we arrive." We told her of our plan to sleep at the bus stop as we had done the night before in Kisumu. "We do not have a lot of money," explained Robert. "We must save what we have to buy food." Malaika nodded but said nothing.

Eventually the sun disappeared below the horizon. But for the yellow beams of the van's headlights illuminating the narrow road ahead, the countryside was completely shrouded in darkness. One by one, most of the passengers, including Robert to my left and Malaika to my right, fell asleep. I tried to sleep, too, but could not. I spent the last hour or so of our journey peering out at the starry sky and the dark outlines of trees, rocks, and the occasional house that flew by the window. I must have dozed off for a few minutes, however, because I was jolted awake by the braking of the van. I opened my eyes and was surprised to see that there were buildings all around us.

Lodwar was larger than we had expected. Although it was nighttime, there were quite a few people and vehicles moving about. As I glanced around, I realized that it might be more difficult to find a quiet place to spend the night here than it had been in Kisumu. As if reading my mind, Malaika interrupted my thoughts. "Please, come to my house," she said. "I live nearby, and I can give you something to eat and a place to sleep tonight." She paused before adding, "I can also show you where to catch the bus to Kakuma in the morning."

I was stunned. From the look on Robert's face, I could tell he was thinking what I was thinking: Why would a young woman invite two strange men to her home? Did she not realize the potential danger? Nevertheless, her invitation was tempting. I had eaten very little all day, so her offer of food was appealing. But before I could say anything, Robert answered for both of us. "Thank you, madam," he said politely. "If it is not too much trouble, we would like something to eat. But after, we can find a place to sleep outside. We will be fine." Malaika smiled and with a wave of her hand, said, "Good. Come along." As she strode ahead of us down the sidewalk, Robert and I looked at each other and shrugged our shoulders simultaneously. We were overjoyed yet filled with disbelief. How could this be happening?

Malaika lived in a small house about a ten-minute walk from the bus stop. She opened the door and ushered us inside. In one corner was a stove, sink, and tiny refrigerator. Several cupboards lined the wall. A small square table and two chairs were within mere millimeters of the refrigerator. Across from the small kitchen were a sofa and another table with a lamp perched on top. Two doors to the right of the kitchen led to a bedroom and to a bathroom, respectively. She invited us to sit down and then disappeared into her bedroom, carrying the bags that she had brought in from the van.

Robert and I sat uncomfortably on the edge of the sofa and waited. She emerged less than a minute later with clean towels and a bag. "I am going to the shop to buy some food to cook for dinner. I will be back soon." Then, pointing to the bathroom door, she continued. "Here, take these towels. You can take a shower while I am gone." With that, she handed us each a towel and washcloth, turned, and walked out the door.

Robert and I were left alone in Malaika's house. We looked at each other nervously.

"Why is she helping us like this?" I asked Robert.

"I don't know," he responded. "I wonder if she's sane."

Nothing about Malaika's behavior during our long bus ride together had suggested that there was anything wrong with her mind. She had seemed perfectly normal and pleasant.

"Maybe she is just naïve," I suggested.

Robert nodded. "You may be right. But if that's the case, then I am glad she met us instead of others who might want to do her harm."

Satisfied for the moment that we were not in danger, Robert headed to the bathroom to clean up. "I barely recognize you," I said, laughing when he emerged twenty minutes later. "You look so clean." It was the first time I had laughed in a long time. I realized how much my spirit had been lifted in anticipation of the meal and by the promise of a full stomach. "Hurry up," responded Robert with a chuckle. "You better be clean, too, before she gets back."

By the time Malaika returned with two large bags of food, both Robert and I had showered and were patiently waiting. We watched as she worked quickly in her small kitchen, and within a short while, dinner was ready. Thankfully, she had bought and cooked a substantial amount of food, so we ate our fill.

After dinner Malaika repeated her earlier offer of a bed for the night. "Lodwar has some of the biggest mosquitoes in all of Kenya," she said with a smile. "It is not wise to sleep outside at all. You will be swollen with mosquito bites by morning. Please spend the night here." Robert and I expressed our thanks for all that she had already done for us, but we insisted on leaving.

"We do not want to inconvenience you," explained Robert.

But Malaika would not hear of it. "Come, bring your bags and follow me," she said.

She rose from the table and led us into her bedroom. "You will both sleep in this bed. See that mosquito net? Don't forget to secure it around the entire bed before you fall asleep, or you will regret it."

Our resolve crumbled at that moment. As incredible as it may seem, Robert and I slept in a complete stranger's comfortable bed under a mosquito net that night, while that stranger slept on a small, uncomfortable sofa in her own living room.

"She must be an angel," I whispered in awe to Robert.

"Yes, indeed," he responded.

The unbelievable dream continued the next morning when we woke to the smell of bacon and eggs cooking in the kitchen. I had not eaten an egg since leaving Rwanda, and I was beyond delighted. After breakfast Malaika led us to the bus stop to catch the van that would take us on the last leg of our trip to the refugee camp in Kakuma. She warned that it could take up to four hours to get there, depending on how many stops we made along the way.

Finally it was time to go. As we struggled to adequately express our gratitude to Malaika, she smiled kindly and said she was happy to have helped us. Then, she wished us a safe journey, waved goodbye, and turned to walk back home. My head spun with questions: Who was this woman? Why had she trusted us? What prompted her excessive and reckless kindness? I remain as perplexed today as I was that morning when we left Lodwar. Perhaps Malaika will read this book one day, seek me out, and provide answers to my questions. Or maybe it was exactly as I suspected—she was an angel whom God had sent to extend hospitality to us along the way.

The terrain changed dramatically as we traveled north, then west between Lodwar and Kakuma. The journey was slow as we traveled up and down several very steep hills. The closer we got to Kakuma, the hotter and drier the air and landscape became. During dinner the night before, Malaika had told us that the region where we were going was dangerous when it rained. Rushing rivers of water would often cascade into the valleys between the hills, washing away everything in their path, including vehicles traveling on the roads that meandered below. She reassured us, however, that the rainy season typically began in April, and it was still only January.

We arrived at the Kakuma Refugee Camp in the afternoon and immediately reported to the United Nations officials in the main office. Two men interviewed us, one of whom was a Kenyan. They spoke with Robert first before turning to ask me questions. As soon as they heard my accent and learned I was Rwandan, their expressions changed. "We cannot allow you into the camp," said the Kenyan official. "If you go in there, you will not survive more than a day or two." I looked toward Robert, hoping for an explanation, but he avoided my gaze. He seemed to understand but was reluctant to say anything to me. "Why would people want to hurt me?" I asked as I turned back to the UN officials.

Though rooted in a complex web of history, politics, and ethnic conflicts, the explanation they gave me was simple and straightforward. They told me that my appearance and accent made it likely that I would be mistaken for a member of the Banyamulenge, a rival ethnic group against whom many of the men in the camp had recently fought in the Zairian war. There was nothing I could do about it.

The officials huddled together to discuss our situation privately for a few minutes before announcing their plan for us. Looking at Robert, the Kenyan official said, "You are from Zaire, and there should be no problem. We will give you what you need to join the others in the camp." Turning to me, he said something completely unexpected. "I have my own residence near the office. You will stay with me there until we can figure out what to do with you next." Then, looking at both of us, he expressed his regret. "I'm very sorry. I know you are friends, but it would probably mean certain death if we were to send you together into the camp." The gravity of his tone left me in no doubt that he was speaking the truth.

When Robert and I went our separate ways that afternoon, we did not know that we would never see each other again. Both he and I assumed we would see each other around the camp since there were no fences or other barriers that separated the staff from the refugees. From where we stood, it appeared that staff residences bordered the camp, so future interactions seemed possible. Maybe he could even stop by the official's residence for an occasional visit, I naively thought. But that was not to be. Soon after moving into the Kenyan official's home, he sat me down and laid down one nonnegotiable rule: "Do not ever leave the house to wander around the grounds by yourself," he instructed. "The men in the camp may see you and…" His voice trailed off. He did not have to finish the sentence. I fully understood the danger.

And so on that very first day at Kakuma Refugee Camp, I said goodbye to my companion Robert, with whom I had traveled so far. I think it was probably a good thing that our relationship ended without me realizing that our separation that afternoon would be permanent. I could not have endured two final farewells in as many days.

PART FIVE
Promises Fulfilled

CHAPTER 16
Miracles

I often mull over unusual or unlikely occurrences and try to make sense of them by asking myself, *Is this coincidence, or is this Jesus's handiwork, designed to achieve a larger purpose?* Through that now-instinctive response, I am able to discern and appreciate how he orchestrates events that harmonize beautifully for my good, how he knits together diverse threads to create the most perfectly designed outcomes for me, and how he opens and closes doors to ensure that I am in the right place at the right time to receive the most exquisite blessings. As I learned to look for and find the hand of Jesus in unusual circumstances during those tumultuous months following my sudden departure from Zaire, my fledgling faith was strengthened.

Nowhere was Jesus's handiwork more obvious to me than during my twenty-one days in Kakuma and the four days that followed immediately afterward. This most remarkable month of my young life all began when the Kenyan official, Mr. Mwangi, issued the surprise invitation to stay in his house. Instead of being forced to live in a camp teeming with people, I had an entire one-bedroom house to myself for most of every day. Mr. Mwangi was a quiet man who generally kept to himself. In the evenings, after he came home from work, we would exchange a few words over the dinner that he would bring for me from the staff cafeteria, and we would occasionally listen to the radio together. Soon he would retreat to his bedroom and close the door, leaving me to my own devices in the small living room. I slept quite comfortably on the sofa with the pillow and blankets he provided. The only other person who entered the house on a regular basis was a woman who came a couple of times each week to clean and do laundry. When we first met, she tried to converse with me, but after she discovered that I spoke no English and that the Swahili I spoke was different from the Swahili that she spoke, she gave up. Other than the occasional smile and greetings we exchanged, she ignored me as she worked.

Having previously lived in a refugee camp, I was most appreciative that Mr. Mwangi allowed me to live in his house. Yet I was also aware that I could not live with him forever. When and where I would move remained a mystery that neither Mr. Mwangi nor the other UN officials seemed able to resolve quickly. For that, I was immensely grateful as I had no desire to move anywhere but to Nairobi.

The heat in Kakuma was unbearable. On one of the few occasions when I ventured outside in the middle of the day, I burned my feet so badly that the scars remained for several years. There was no air conditioner, and during the day, the house was only marginally cooler than the outside. At night it was the exact opposite. The air turned extremely cold, and I was thankful for the extra blanket on the sofa. Regardless of the weather, because of Mr. Mwangi's warning about the men in the camp, I rarely ventured into the small yard in front of the house, and even then, only when he was at home.

With no one to speak to and nothing else to do all day, I began to read my Bible voraciously. I would read and reread passages that were difficult to understand and would commit to memory those that resonated with my spirit. Among my favorites were these:

> The righteous person faces many troubles, but the Lord comes to the rescue each time. For the Lord protects the bones of the righteous; not one of them is broken. (Psalm 34:19–20)

> The Lord directs the steps of the godly. He delights in every detail of their lives. (Psalm 37:23)

> We are pressed on every side by troubles, but we are not crushed. We are perplexed, but not driven to despair. We are hunted down, but never abandoned by God. We get knocked down, but we are not destroyed. (2 Corinthians 4:8–9)

> For God has said, "I will never fail you. I will never abandon you." (Hebrews 13:5)

With no one to help me interpret and apply the scriptures to my life, I would often ask God to help me understand what I was reading. And he did. I was amazed at the revelation that came with repetition. I was particularly intrigued by the power of prayer and was captivated by biblical accounts of the men and women who had called out to God and had their prayers answered. Their great faith and perseverance were not lost on me and neither was the fact that many fasted as they prayed. And so after the first few days, I not only read my Bible and prayed, but I periodically fasted as well.

Years later I would ask myself how it was that at age seventeen I had developed the attention span and intense desire to fast, pray, and read my Bible, almost unceasingly, for so many hours every day, for twenty-one days straight. Without a doubt, the answer could be attributed to the absence of distractions. I had no family, no friends, no home, no school, no money, and almost no personal belongings. All I owned was a Bible, a school identification card, and the secondhand clothes that Mr. Mwangi had graciously given me when he realized that the garments I had brought with me from Zaire were no longer wearable. Nor could I imagine a future. There was no obvious path forward for me. If ever a person was alone in the world and facing a dead end, it was me. I felt miserable and hopeless.

But soon my mindset changed. I developed a sense of gratitude and appreciation for the little that I did have. I came to believe that Jesus had arranged this period of seclusion so that I could get to know him better and to understand what it means to rely on him and him alone. It was the only thing that made sense to me. Why else would I have suddenly found myself in a remote corner of Kenya, in a clean, comfortable, and safe house, with enough food to eat and all the time in the world to converse with my Lord without interruption? It was as if Jesus himself had carried me and deposited me in Mr. Mwangi's house—an oasis of plenty and safety in the middle of a desert of scarcity and danger that surrounded me in the refugee camp and in the arid countryside beyond the gates of the camp. And although all was not well in my life, I was still able to appreciate the unexpected gift of Mr. Mwangi's home through the intense pain that I continued to endure. Seeing the silver lining in my situation helped me enormously.

Each day I would call out to Jesus in desperation. He did not answer me suddenly or immediately, as some people may have experienced. Rather, it was gradual. Over time he reached into my emptiness and filled me with his Holy Presence and a sense of peace that made no sense to me. My external condition and circumstances had not changed—I was still alone with no resources or future—so there was nothing that should have produced a sense of peace. It was only later in my walk of faith that I would learn about the peace "which exceeds anything we can understand."[1] That was exactly the kind of peace I experienced sitting there in the middle of the floor in Mr. Mwangi's living room. It is hard to explain, but as I communed with Jesus daily, I gradually began to feel more confident, less afraid, and more empowered. I began to believe that the promises of God that I read about in the Bible were indeed written for me, even though my way forward in life was completely unclear at the moment.

Even now, I rejoice and give thanks for those twenty-one days—days that were so special that I counted and remembered the exact number. Without that period of peace, quiet, and rest, I may have physically collapsed from the exhaustion of traveling long distances under stressful conditions and living in physically uncomfortable surroundings. Or worse, I may have spiritually stagnated in a superficial relationship with Jesus. Without this extended period of fasting and prayer, I may never have developed the spiritual wisdom and insight to pray an all-important prayer—one I repeated daily while in Kakuma: *Lord, if you get me out of here, I will serve you for the rest of my life.*

It was late in the afternoon on the twenty-first day that I saw the large, turquoise-colored truck. I had stepped outside to stretch my legs after a morning of intense prayer on the floor of Mr. Mwangi's living room. It was the time of day when many trucks arrived at the camp to drop off food, medicine, and other supplies. There were close to fifty huge trucks in the large lot. Some drivers were lined up to drop off their load, while others had already unloaded and were parked in designated areas of the compound. The drivers would spend the night at the camp rather than attempting a return trip in the dark. Safety was a major concern, and the Kenyan military prohibited nighttime travel in the region. The turquoise truck caught my eye because of its unusual color, which reminded me of the trucks I used to see on the streets of Kigali. I looked at it more closely, and to my surprise and delight, I saw that it did indeed have a Rwandan license plate!

I had not expected to meet any Rwandans this far north, and I was immediately curious as to the identity of the driver. Soon I saw a very tall and muscular man emerge from one of the nearby buildings and begin to stroll around the vehicle, peering at the tires. I walked over to him and greeted him in the Rwandan language, Kinyarwanda. "Hello! Is everything okay with the truck?" The man looked up suddenly. It was clear he had not expected to hear anyone speaking Kinyarwanda in Kakuma.

Over the next few minutes, I learned that he was the truck driver and his name was Caleb. Both he and his codriver, Gahigi, were from Kigali. "My boss has a contract with the World Food Program, and I deliver the supplies to the refugee camps," he explained. "We are heading back to Nairobi tomorrow morning to pick up another load."

Nairobi! I must have gasped audibly when he said the word because he looked at me strangely for a moment before asking, "Why are you surprised to hear I am going to Nairobi?"

My words tumbling out in excitement, I told Caleb about the Patrick family and my plan to meet up with them in Nairobi. "Can you take me to them?" I asked eagerly.

Caleb shook his head. "I'm sorry, but there are rules," he said. "I am not allowed to take anyone away from the camps."

"No one will know," I insisted. "I can hide in the back of the truck." I then went on to explain that I was staying at Mr. Mwangi's house and how dangerous it was for me at the camp. "Please help me; I have to get away from here," I pleaded. "There is no life for me in this camp. The men here want to kill me."

Caleb hesitated, peering into my face as if trying to determine whether I was telling the truth. "What is your name?" he said finally. "I don't know anything about you."

"My name is Jean Bosco Gapfizi," I responded politely. "I am the oldest son of my father."

Caleb stared hard at me. His expression was inscrutable. "Did you say Gapfizi?" he asked. I nodded. His eyes narrowed as he followed up with another question. "Where is your father now?"

And so I felt compelled to tell Caleb my story. It was raw and painful to share with a stranger, and I felt he was somehow invading my privacy. But if that was what it took to convince him to take me with him to Nairobi, then I would have to tell him.

I explained how I had been separated from my parents in Kigali when the genocide began and how I was forced to run into the forest. I told him how the Patrick family took me to Zaire and how I later learned that my entire family had been killed. I ended with the story of my escape to Uganda and my journey across the Kenyan border to Kisumu and then to Kakuma. I did not share all the details—I kept the emotional pain of the past year to myself as best I could. I told him only what I thought would be enough to satisfy his curiosity and hopefully convince him to help me. When I finished speaking, Caleb was silent for what seemed like an eternity.

"All right," he said at last. "I will take you, but you will need to figure out a way to get past the guards at the gate. They will search every inch of my truck before I leave here."

I was elated, and for a moment, I could not believe what I was hearing. "Thank you so much," I said. "Just tell me what time you plan to leave in the morning. I will figure out a way to get through the gates. Perhaps we can meet near the shops?" We conversed for a few more minutes about the details of my plan. Reassured that he meant to help me, I said good night and headed back to the house.

Mr. Mwangi was reading at the dining table when I entered the living room. I was breathless, having raced from the truck back to the house. I could barely curb my excitement as I told him about Caleb and his promise to take me to my friends in Nairobi. Mr. Mwangi was stunned at this sudden and surprising development, but I could tell he was also relieved. I had been in the camp for three weeks, and he had still not yet figured out what to do with me. Caleb's offer was an answer to a seemingly intractable problem. After all, it was plausible that because Caleb was Rwandan and was well-connected to the Rwandan community in Nairobi, he would be able to locate the Patricks and deliver me to them.

"What time is this truck driver planning to leave?" he asked.

"He told me to be in front of the shops outside the gate no later than seven thirty tomorrow morning," I responded.

Mr. Mwangi glanced at his watch, sprang to his feet, and headed for the door. "I'll be back in fifteen minutes," he said rather mysteriously as the door closed behind him. He returned ten minutes later, waving a piece of paper in his hand. "This will allow you to walk out of the gates in the morning," he explained. "It's a temporary pass. I am authorized to approve it. Show it to the guards, and they will not question you."

I took the pass and thanked Mr. Mwangi. "This is all I need," I assured him. "Caleb has a plan to hide me in his truck. I will make it to Nairobi."

Early the next morning, I said goodbye to Mr. Mwangi and

expressed my appreciation. I told him that what he had done for me went far beyond the responsibilities of someone in his position, and I promised that I would never forget his kindness.

"It was my pleasure to help you, Bosco," he responded. "Be careful in Nairobi. It's a big city, and it is easy to lose your way there." As he wished me a safe journey and shook my hand one last time, he placed a few Kenyan shillings in my palm. "You may want to purchase a couple of samosas to eat along the way," he said with a smile.

I walked out of the Kakuma Refugee Camp minutes later with my small bag of belongings slung over my left shoulder and my temporary pass clutched in my right hand. The guards at the gate scrutinized the authorization form before handing it back to me and waving me through. I was so excited I almost ran down the road toward the shops. About five minutes later, I heard the unmistakable sound of a truck coming up the road behind me. It pulled up alongside me and came to a grinding halt, and the large, turquoise-blue door swung open. Caleb stepped out and gestured for me to climb in. "Move toward the back, behind the seats, and lie down under the bed. We'll be pulling up to the first roadblock in a few minutes." There was another man sitting in the truck, but there was no time to say hello as Caleb nervously told me to hurry. "Quick, we don't want anyone to see you!"

The police officers at the first checkpoint seemed to know Caleb from his previous visits to the camp. They greeted each other cheerfully, and the officers only gave a cursory glance into the back of the truck, no doubt aware that a more thorough search had just been conducted at the gate of the refugee camp. Once we passed through that first checkpoint, Caleb called out in a loud voice, "You can sit up front with us now, Bosco. I want you to meet Gahigi." I said hello to Caleb's assistant as I climbed into the front and took a seat between the two men. Gahigi did not respond immediately. It was obvious that he was surprised, and he looked questioningly at me and then at Caleb. "We are taking this boy to Nairobi to meet his friends," said Caleb casually. "It will be all right." Gahigi appeared unconvinced. He glanced at me suspiciously before nodding a halfhearted greeting. He then turned his attention to the road ahead.

I was just beginning to relax and enjoy the surrounding scenery when the interrogation began. "So you said your name is Gapfizi? What was your father's first name, and what was your mother's first name?" Caleb's tone was unnerving, and I began to feel alarmed. I thought I had given him all the relevant information he needed the night before, but I was wrong. For twenty minutes Caleb questioned me about the neighborhood where I use to live and the address of our compound. He asked about the work my father did and even about the employees who use to work for him. His demeanor was intense, intrusive, and aggressive. Did he not believe what I was telling him? My apprehension grew.

What did I really know about this large and imposing man or his traveling companion? I recalled some of the stories I had heard from the Patrick family about long-distance truck drivers. That they were not all good people. That many engaged in criminal activity as they drove from town to town because it was easy for them to evade capture. I glanced at Caleb out of the corner of my eye. He was tall and very muscular. Gahigi was shorter, but he too appeared to be very strong. I was completely at their mercy. A bead of sweat formed near my throat, and I felt it trickle down my chest before being absorbed into my shirt. The sweat on my brow was not entirely due to the heat. I was afraid. Mr. Mwangi was the only person in the world who knew I had boarded this truck with these two men, but it was unlikely he would recall their names or even what they looked like. When we parted, we both assumed we would never see each other again. How would he possibly know whether I made it to Nairobi or not? The sad truth was there was no one on earth who would miss me if I were to disappear. The pain that accompanied that realization was so powerful that it momentarily distracted me from the possibility that I was in mortal danger.

"Give me your school identification card!" Caleb's abrupt command jolted me back to the present. My fingers shook as I opened my small bag to retrieve the card. As I struggled to complete that simple task, my imagination ran wild. Did he want my identification card so he could destroy evidence of who I was before he and his companion killed me? Would he then dump me along a lonely stretch of road where wild animals would devour my body before it could be found? I found the card and handed it over to him. Without slowing the vehicle, Caleb took his eyes off the road momentarily to glance at the card. His expression did not change, but he became quiet. I wanted to ask him to return it to me, but I was reluctant to break the silence.

For the next five minutes, no one spoke. Suddenly, without any warning whatsoever, Caleb pressed on the brakes and steered the truck off the road into a grassy patch that extended for several meters. My body stiffened as I hastily planned my escape. The truck had a back door, so I would leap over the seat as soon as we stopped and quickly exit through the rear. I was young and fast and confident that I could outrun my criminal companions. They would not be able to catch me before I reached the wooded area in the distance. The brush was thick. I would hide there. It would be my only way out of this predicament.

The truck came to a halt, and then, just as I turned to jump over the seat, Caleb said five words that stopped me in my tracks.

"You look like your mother."

I stared at him in disbelief. Thoughts of escape faded in an instant. I opened my mouth to speak, but before I could utter a sound, Caleb launched into his story.

"As soon as you told me your name was Gapfizi back at the camp, I thought it might be you, but I needed to make sure. That's why I asked so many questions. When you were a young child, your father hired me to be his driver, and I worked with him for several years. He was a good man. Your mother was beautiful. She was very kind to me." I was flabbergasted. Caleb then went on to describe the exact location of my father's business, as well as details about our home and some of the other employees, proving beyond any shadow of a doubt that he knew me and my family.

I sat in stunned silence, not sure what to feel. Astonishment, grief, relief all competed for supremacy. On the one hand, I could hardly believe what I was hearing. I was traveling with someone who had known and respected my parents! But the memories he shared about them stirred up the pain that was never far away. But there was joy as well. Jesus had come through for me again with yet another miracle. Of all the truck drivers in Kenya, how could it be that this one, sent to Kakuma on that day in February 1997, knew me and my family? And how was it that I happened to be standing outside at just the right moment to see the Rwandan license plate on Caleb's truck? No, my faith did not allow me to believe that it could have been simple coincidence. Jesus had orchestrated events, yet again, in my favor. I was convinced of it.

And as if that was not enough good news for one day, Caleb delivered even more. "My boss in Nairobi knew your father too," he said. "When I tell him who you are, he will be so surprised. I believe he will be able to help you to find the Patrick family. Until you do, I am sure he will allow you to stay with him. Do not worry, young man; everything will be okay."

As he restarted the truck and pulled back onto the road, I felt physically lighter. The burden of fear that I had felt moments before had been lifted from my shoulders, and the tightness in my chest was released. I could breathe freely, and for the first time in as far back as I could remember, the tears that welled up in my eyes were tears of joy. As much as I had wanted to believe the promises of Jesus as I had fasted and prayed during my time in Mr. Mwangi's home, I had continued to have moments of doubt. I was only human, still a child in the faith, both literally and figuratively.

Now, as I swayed along in harmony with the rocking of the truck, I was reminded of the Ugandan pastor's instruction to delay going to Nairobi and to head north to Kakuma instead. Through that pastor, Jesus had steered me to the exact place he had wanted me to be. While it may not have been the shortest route to Nairobi, it certainly turned out to be the *best* way to go. By going to Nairobi via a one-month detour to faraway Kakuma, I had found someone who was willing to help me and even provide shelter and food for me in Nairobi. I was filled with excitement and anticipation. Hope had returned.

CHAPTER 17

Lost No More

I was surprised to learn that the 730-kilometer drive from Kakuma to Nairobi would take us approximately four days. "There are several towns along the way," Caleb assured me, "so we won't have to sleep in the truck." I hesitated to reveal my financial situation but decided it was best to do so sooner rather than later. "I have no money," I said quietly. "I will sleep in the truck." Caleb looked at me and smiled. "I have enough money to pay for whatever you need, Bosco. Your father was good to me, and I am happy to help you now."

But while everything seemed to be going better than I could ever have hoped, there was one major concern with which we would have to contend repeatedly on our journey: roadblocks. As part of an effort by the Kenyan police to promote safety and security on the roads, vehicles were stopped for quick safety inspections and passengers questioned at seemingly random locations along the road between many of the towns. "I have traveled these roads often enough, and I know where most of the roadblocks are usually set up," Caleb said confidently. "I will warn you beforehand so you can hide in the back. We will be fine."

Sure enough, on that first day, we passed through two additional roadblocks. On both occasions Caleb gave me a ten-minute warning, and I hid under the small bed in the back of the truck before we arrived at the barrier. Gahigi then threw an assortment of items on and around the bed to make it look as if the area had not been disturbed in a while. At each roadblock I barely breathed as I listened to Caleb and Gahigi greet the officers. And when the officers opened the door to peer inside the back of the truck, I feared they would hear the pounding of my heart. After the second such terrifying experience, Caleb called out to me, "You can come on up front now, Bosco. Relax; there will be no more checkpoints today. The next one is several kilometers past the village where we will be sleeping tonight."

Late in the evening, we pulled into a small town. Caleb parked the truck near a guesthouse and announced we would spend the night there. We were hungry and immediately took a seat in the café next door. After a big dinner, Gahigi rose and announced he was going to put some gas in the truck so that it would be ready when we left early in the morning. As he left, Caleb explained that Gahigi would sleep in the truck to make sure no one stole any of its parts or the personal items locked up inside.

Caleb rented a spacious room for us in the guesthouse. There were two small beds, neither of which looked large enough to accommodate Caleb's substantial frame. After washing up in the bathroom down the hallway, Caleb returned to our room and threw himself onto one of the beds. Though he lay diagonally, his massive feet still hung over the edge. It did not seem to bother him, however. Within a minute his steady, hard breathing indicated that he was sound asleep.

I crawled between the sheets of my own bed, but my eyes refused to close. I lay there, marveling at the day's unexpected turn of events. Fewer than forty-eight hours earlier, I could not have imagined myself in these surroundings, on my way to Nairobi with a family acquaintance who had vowed to help me find the Patrick family. Before falling asleep, I whispered a short prayer: "Lord, only you know the future. Into your hands I place my life. Give me the faith to trust you for tomorrow and for whatever comes my way."

The next morning we rose early and left town just as the sun was rising. We drove in silence for about an hour before Gahigi spoke. "I can't remember whether it was at the next roadblock or the one after that." He paused. "But the last time we drove through here, the police climbed up into the truck and searched thoroughly. I am afraid that if they do that again, they might find the boy." Gahigi was a quiet man. He had said little since I met him, so the fact that he was speaking up now surprised me. I concluded that he must have been really worried and that his anxiety was warranted. We both looked at Caleb for a response.

"You may be right," he acknowledged. "Why don't you both get out and walk together past the next roadblock? The authorities will just think you are a father and son walking from your farm to a neighbor's farm or to the next village. I don't think they will bother you. It's the vehicular traffic they are really interested in checking out." Then with a grin, he turned to me and added, "Just don't say a word, Bosco. You do not sound like a Kenyan!"

About half an hour later, Caleb pulled over. "The roadblock is coming up soon," he said. "Get out here and keep walking along the side of the road. I will wait here for about twenty minutes before continuing. Once you pass the checkpoint, keep walking until you are out of view of the police. I will pick you up on the other side."

The plan worked perfectly. The police officers hardly even looked at us as we strolled past. I was relieved to see other pedestrians in the distance. Caleb was right. The sight of a father and son walking together in broad daylight was not unusual. Gahigi waved at the three officers who were monitoring the roadway, but I kept my eyes straight ahead. I did not want them to see the fear in my eyes. Neither of us said a word.

Later, when Caleb drove up alongside us, we quickly climbed back into the truck, secure in the knowledge that we were out of view of the officers. As we pulled away, I leaned back and closed my eyes. Only then did I allow sweet relief to wash over me.

The third day of our trip to Nairobi was much like the first two days. We rose early and, after a hearty breakfast, began driving. I was no longer nervous about walking past the roadblocks. The police had no interest in speaking to Gahigi or me and barely acknowledged our presence when we strolled by. In fact, so confident had I become that a couple of times I walked past the roadblocks all by myself. It was an opportunity to stretch my legs and get a little exercise. I also enjoyed the solitude of these brief walks. The truck's cabin was small, and I was not comfortable sitting in such close proximity to Caleb and Gahigi for hours and hours. Although they were pleasant and thankfully not very talkative, they were strangers, and I looked forward to the chance to be alone with my thoughts.

I don't know whether it was because Caleb was tired and had lost track of where we were or because the roadblock was set up in an unexpected location, but toward evening we rounded a bend in the road and were shocked to find ourselves face-to-face with several police officers. It was too late for me to either hide or exit the vehicle. I could see one of the officers looking directly at me. I froze, but Caleb leaped into action. Rather than waiting for the officers to approach the truck, he parked, jumped down, and strode toward them.

Caleb never did tell me what he said to those men. It seemed he spoke with them for hours, but it was probably not more than a few minutes. When he returned to the truck, he avoided my gaze and simply turned the key in the ignition. Then, at the direction of one of the officers who lifted the barrier, we slowly drove through and continued on our way. I glanced at Caleb's profile as he stared ahead. Tension was evident in every muscle of his face. It was only then that I realized just how narrowly we had averted disaster.

That terrifying moment reminded me of just how vulnerable I was and how much my future, indeed my very life, was dependent on these two strangers with whom I was traveling. But hadn't this been the case for the past few months, if not years? I had been like a sailboat without a rudder, subject to every sudden wind that blew me in an unexpected direction. It was as if my life was not my own. Everyone but me was in control. It was an awful feeling.

But even as I wallowed in self-pity, the Holy Spirit himself opened my eyes and spoke to my heart. The people into whose arms I had been "blown" included Francois, who saved my life in the forest; the Patricks, who provided a safe home for me and treated me as their very own when my family was gone; my friend Kwima and Pastor Isaiah, who introduced me to Jesus; Habimana and Sentwali, who brought me safely, and against all odds, from Zaire to Kenya; the Ugandan pastor who provided me wise counsel; Robert, my friend, who helped relieve my loneliness; Malaika, the stranger who provided food and shelter in Lodwar; Mr. Mwangi, who protected me and facilitated my escape from the Kakuma camp; and Caleb, who had now assumed the role of my guardian and protector. Every one of these individuals had worked on my behalf and for my good. At that moment I realized the truth that had somehow escaped me up until then: I had not been tossed and blown by random winds; I had been lovingly guided and directed by the very breath of Jesus.

The fourth day dawned bright and sunny. Caleb had announced over breakfast that we would be arriving in Nairobi by early afternoon. Finally! The city I had dreamed about going to for so long was only a few hours away. I felt a twinge of sadness as I thought about Robert, who had shared this dream. I had not been able to tell him goodbye. Now I wondered how he was doing. I prayed he was safe and that one day he, too, would make it to Nairobi. But I would not know. After leaving Kakuma, I never saw Robert again.

As we neared Nairobi, Gahigi and Caleb debated the pros and cons of taking one of two possible routes into the city. They eventually decided on a less-traveled back route that would take a little longer than the alternative but would likely have less traffic. We had already left the countryside behind us, and the area through which we were now driving was gradually becoming more congested with vehicles, people, and buildings. Suddenly Caleb pointed to a woman standing on the sidewalk. He blew the truck's horn, and she turned and waved when she saw the truck. "I'll be right back," said Caleb as he parked the truck and jumped out. "I need to talk to her." A minute or two later, Gahigi announced that he was going into a nearby store. "If Caleb returns before I do, tell him I won't be long."

Sitting alone in the truck, I looked around. People seemed to be in a hurry, and I found myself gazing at the faces of those who scurried around in front of the truck. That was when I saw him. He was weaving in and out of the traffic as he crossed the street. His movements caught my attention. They looked familiar. At first, I thought I was mistaken, so I sat up and leaned against the windscreen to be sure. It *was* him! It was Gael, Mr. Patrick's oldest son. The very person I had thought I might spend months looking for in Nairobi was right in front of me! I reacted instantaneously, unlocking the truck door and sliding to the ground in one movement. I ran at breakneck speed to catch up with him before he disappeared into the crowd. Within seconds I was standing directly behind him. "Gael!" I shouted. He swung around, and I will never forget the look on his face. It was as if he was looking at a ghost. "Bosco? Is that really you?" His voice was a whisper. I rushed forward and embraced him.

When I tell people how I found the Patrick family within minutes of entering the city, many shake their heads in disbelief. I understand completely. In 1997 the population of Nairobi was almost two million. Finding a member of the Patrick family in that city, without an address or phone number, was like finding the proverbial needle in the haystack. But to anyone who doubts the power of Jesus to orchestrate such a miraculous meeting, I would remind you about how Jesus fed five thousand people with a few fish and pieces of bread, walked on water, calmed a storm with his words, and performed innumerable other miracles, including rising from the dead after his crucifixion. Given all that, what Jesus did that day in a neighborhood called Kawangware on the outskirts of Nairobi is certainly within his power and grace.

And so just like that, my journey with Caleb and Gahigi came to an end. I no longer needed their help. I introduced them to Gael and explained that he was Mr. Patrick's son. Both men greeted him warmly and expressed their astonishment at our improbable encounter. "My boss will never believe this," exclaimed Caleb, shaking his head. "You are a lucky boy, Bosco," he said with a laugh. I smiled. If only he knew. It had nothing to do with luck at all. After saying goodbye to Caleb and Gahigi and promising to stay in touch, I headed off down the road with Gael toward my new home.

The other Patrick children were just as shocked to see me as Gael had been. Having heard about the terrible war in Zaire, they had feared

I had been killed. But now, within only a matter of hours of arriving in Nairobi, I was completely settled in with Gael; his brothers Jean-Claude and Dido; and his sisters Honorine, Olive, and Isaro. Space was limited, but no one seemed to mind sharing with one more. I took a hot shower, after which they took me to get a haircut, new clothes, and new shoes. I felt like a new person both inside and out.

After dinner that night, we chatted for hours. They wanted to hear about everything that had happened to me since we had parted ways, and they hung on my every word. I was interrupted only by the occasional gasp as I recounted the unbelievable turn of events that had brought me from Zaire into their living room in Nairobi. "God is good!" Honorine exclaimed over and over as she savored each detail. The others nodded vigorously in agreement.

In the days and weeks that followed, I reveled in my newfound freedom to eat as much as I wanted, to again read books and magazines, and to turn on a radio or television at any time. It was all so strange but in the most wonderful way. I knew I would eventually go back to school, but I was in no hurry, and to my surprise, the others did not raise the issue. Their reluctance may have had to do with the fact that I lacked the proper identification documents, but at the time, I did not know or care. Having lived in rural areas for such a long time, I found Nairobi to be quite exciting, and when not reading or watching television, I would explore the city for hours on end. One or more of the Patrick children accompanied me at first, but it was not long before I was able to venture out comfortably on my own.

I quickly discovered that it was imperative for me to speak English and Kenyan-style Swahili, so I began studying both. Fortunately I had a knack for languages, and so just as I had easily learned French at school in Rwanda and Swahili in Zaire, I began to rapidly acquire these two new languages.

Lack of money was not a problem. Shortly after I had arrived so unexpectedly, the Patrick children had sent word to their father back in Rwanda that I was now living with them. He was happy to hear that I was alive and responded by sending additional funds to help ensure that all my needs would be met. It was most difficult to contain the joy that bubbled up inside of me every day as I considered how drastically my circumstances had changed for the better.

My life of pleasure and freedom in Nairobi continued uninterrupted for about two months. Then one day the inconceivable and unexpected happened once again. It was the middle of the afternoon, and I was at home with Isaro and Jean-Claude when there was a loud knock on the door. Jean-Claude approached the door tentatively and asked, "Who is it?"

The response shocked us all. "This is the police! Open up the door now!" Isaro and I remained frozen in our chairs as Jean-Claude fumbled with the lock. Within seconds three burly police officers strode into the center of the living room and started to ask questions.

Even before the first police officer spoke, I knew why they had come. A few days earlier, I had been listening to the news on the radio and heard a disturbing announcement. The Kenyan government had decided to launch a concerted effort to round up all refugees who were living in the city illegally. Refugees who had valid permits would be allowed to remain, but everyone else would be arrested immediately. I tried to reassure myself that I lived in a house, wore nice clothes, and so I did not fit the image of a poor, dirty, homeless refugee. From all appearances, I was a typical middle-class Kenyan teenager. I had not for one moment anticipated that the authorities would enter our home. But there they were.

Jean-Claude and Isaro presented their permits to the police officers for inspection. After returning the permits to them, the officers turned to me. I showed them my school identification card from Zaire, which was the only document I possessed. "This is not valid," said the first officer as he handed it back to me. "Where is your permit?" It did not take them long to discover that I was in Nairobi illegally. My accent and missing travel documents were all the proof they needed. They told Isaro and Jean-Claude the name of the police station where they would be taking me before beckoning me to walk outside with them. I barely had time to push my Bible into my pocket before they ushered me out the front door and into the back of the police Jeep. The entire episode happened in the blink of an eye.

Once again my life had changed in an instant. I could barely breathe. After all I had gone through to get to Nairobi, was it all going to come crashing down like this? *If they send me to prison, I will surely die,* I thought.

I was placed in a cell at the police station with some fifteen other men. I stayed there for four interminable days. There was only one other man who, like me, had been arrested for entering the country illegally. All the others were in jail for an assortment of crimes that they sometimes boasted about. I was the youngest person in the cell, and I was very afraid of the other men. I tried my best to stay out of their way, to speak as little as possible, and not to draw any attention to myself.

The living conditions in that cell were the worst I had ever seen or endured. There were no chairs or beds or even mats on the floor. It was just a room with bare concrete floors and walls. In one corner was a single toilet that everyone used in full view of everyone else. I believed it had not been cleaned in months. There was no window. The only ventilation was a small rectangular opening in the wall near the ceiling. The walls were very thick, and one could neither see nor hear anything from outside.

Gael and Jean-Claude came to visit and bring me food and a bottle of milk every day. I would swallow it gratefully in a few gulps. The police provided no food to any of the inmates, and everyone was very hungry. But for these daily ten-minute visits, I would have starved. The only other act of kindness I experienced in that place came in the form of advice from one of the guards on my very first day. "When your family comes to visit, eat everything they bring for you while you are with them out front. If you take any food back to the cell, the other men will expect you to share it with them. And if you don't, that could mean trouble for you." And so each day, I would hurriedly consume whatever Gael and Jean-Claude brought during their visit. There was little time for conversation, which was just as well. They had no idea how to help me.

On the morning of the fourth day, a police officer escorted me and several of the other men in my cell to court. When it was my turn to stand before the judge, I stepped forward. I listened but said nothing. I did not understand what was happening as they spoke in English. The proceeding lasted only a couple of minutes and ended with someone, I don't recall whom, translating the judge's words: "Your court date is in two weeks. In the meantime you will go to prison."

Prison. The word rang loudly and painfully in my ear. I wanted to scream. Would anyone come to rescue me from this nightmare I was now living? I called out to Jesus in my mind: *Why would you bless me by bringing me safely and so miraculously to Nairobi and to the Patrick family to then, only weeks later, snatch my blessing back? Why is this happening to me, Lord?* Jesus was silent.

"Let's go! This way." The guard's loud voice interrupted my thoughts. He motioned for me to follow him through a door that led to a parking lot at the back of the building. There I boarded a bus that was already half full of other inmates. We waited a few minutes for a couple more inmates to board, and then the door closed. The bus had no windows, so I closed my eyes. I was on my way to a Kenyan prison, just as the Ugandan pastor had feared might happen.

CHAPTER 18

Destiny Revealed

I was assigned to one of five barracks that each housed roughly one hundred men. Rows of mattresses were arranged on the floor, and the guards pointed me to one that was available. They did not give me a sheet or pillow, and the mattress was absolutely filthy. It was obvious that many men had slept on it before me. But I had no choice—it was either the mattress or the even-dirtier floor.

Life during those fourteen days revolved around two unsatisfying meals each day. Every morning we took a shower in cold water before being led out into the courtyard for breakfast. The inmates who were still awaiting trial were separated from the others, but we were all made to squat low to the ground in a large outdoor plaza while we ate. We had no table, chairs, or utensils other than a tin cup and plate. We ate with our hands. Breakfast always consisted of a thin porridge, and dinner always included cooked cornmeal, or ugali, and so-called cabbage soup. On those few days that I found a single cabbage leaf in my "soup," I considered myself to be quite fortunate. Each inmate kept his own bowl and cup and brought both to the courtyard where the food was distributed. I cannot remember how or if we ever washed them. It's likely they did not need to be cleaned because we were always so hungry that not a single morsel was left behind. Or maybe we rinsed them in the showers each morning. Regardless, I kept a close eye on my cup and plate. Without them, I would be given nothing to eat.

During one quiet moment of reflection late at night in the prison barracks, I recalled that soon after arriving in Nairobi, I had ceased to read my Bible and pray with the intensity and devotion that I had exhibited in Kakuma. In fact, since I had arrived in Nairobi, there had been entire days during which I neither read my Bible nor prayed. I was too busy enjoying myself. It was difficult to admit, but I could not deny the truth. As soon as I got what I wanted, I began to neglect he who had made it all possible. But now here I was in prison, and once again I was reading my Bible and praying intensely for help to get me out of my current predicament.

I felt ashamed that the faith I proclaimed was so shallow. My life had become more about what Jesus could do for me than about true worship and service to others. So while in prison, I asked Jesus to forgive me for seeking to cultivate my relationship with him only when I wanted him to act on my behalf. I then decided to repeat the prayer that I had prayed in Kakuma: *Lord, if you get me out of this, I will serve you.* But this time I asked him to help me fulfill that faith promise. At that moment I realized that I could do nothing in my own strength—not even follow through on a simple promise. But if I acknowledged my own weakness and instead relied on *his* power, I could accomplish anything.

Finally my court date arrived. I joined several other inmates in the rear of a small, windowless truck for the thirty-minute drive back to the courthouse. The dozen or so tiny holes that had been drilled into the side of the truck, just above our heads, barely provided sufficient air for the bodies inside. It was a miserable trip. As I waited in the courthouse hallway for my name to be called, I shuffled my feet nervously and wiped my moist palms repeatedly on the legs of my pants. And I silently prayed with a fervor that caused me to sweat. *Lord, please help me. I don't want to spend five years in prison.*

"Bosco!" A familiar voice interrupted my prayer. I looked up to see Gael hurrying toward me, an anxious expression on his face. "They told me your court date is today. I really wanted to see you," he explained with a weak smile.

"Thank you," I whispered. I was happy he had come, but in a strange way, his presence made me even more acutely aware of my loneliness. We stood, side by side, in an uncomfortable silence, both fearful of what would happen next.

"Jean Bosco Gapfizi!" The guard's voice was loud and clear. A second guard took me by the arm and led me into the courtroom. Gael followed closely behind. "I will translate and explain everything that is said," he had promised me moments earlier. I was relieved. My limited understanding of the proceedings two weeks before, during my first trip to the court, had exacerbated my growing sense of vulnerability.

My knees were shaking as I approached the judge. Looking directly into my eyes, the judge began to speak, and almost simultaneously Gael whispered her words to me in Kinyarwanda, our native language. He told me that because I was an unaccompanied minor, a child in the eyes of the court, the judge was not going to sentence me to prison. I was so weak with relief that my knees began to buckle beneath me. Desperately focused on regaining my balance, I almost missed hearing the second, even more important decision of the court, which Gael declared breathlessly, his words practically tumbling out of his mouth: "You have been granted asylum and will be released immediately. You may continue to reside in Kenya." He paused briefly to listen to the judge again, then declared in astonishment: "You can go and collect your permit right now!"

Gael gripped my shoulders excitedly from behind, and I turned to look at him, stunned and barely able to move. "Are you sure?" I was afraid to believe what he had told me. He flung his head back and laughed in response.

I felt like a wanderer who had finally entered the Promised Land. This time, however, I would not forget my Lord, Jesus Christ, who had mercifully choreographed both people and events to ensure my safe arrival. A trip to prison had helped me to learn that important lesson, and from that day forward, I have never stopped making my relationship with Jesus my number-one priority—both in good times and bad.

But it was not only the judge's ruling that led me to recommit to a life of faith that would not be swayed by circumstances. It was also the realization that my arrest, at age seventeen, was actually a blessing in disguise. Had the police arrested me later on, when I was no longer a minor, the court would not likely have ruled in my favor. I believe that Jesus in his infinite wisdom arranged for me to be arrested at seventeen to ensure that I would be eligible to remain in Kenya permanently and not have to constantly hide in the shadows as an illegal refugee. My arrest at that precise time was the best thing that could have happened to me, although I was completely blind to that fact at the time. Once again Jesus poured out his favor on my life in a most perplexing yet perfect way, highlighting the truth of scripture that says: "'My thoughts are nothing like your thoughts,' says the Lord. 'And my ways are far beyond anything you could imagine. For just as the heavens are higher than the earth, so my ways are higher than your ways, and my thoughts higher than your thoughts.'"[1]

I returned to the Patrick home as a legal resident of Kenya. The others were so happy to see me it felt like a celebratory homecoming. Shortly afterward I enrolled in high school, and for the first time since leaving Zaire, I began to live a normal life, with Mr. Patrick continuing to cover all of my personal and academic expenses and his children treating me like a beloved younger brother. I went to school, did my homework, played sports, went to church, and made new friends. I felt settled and secure—financially, physically, socially, and above all, spiritually.

One group of friends was particularly special. They included several teens who were from Rwanda, like me, and Burundi, the country of my former music teacher in grade seven. Every Saturday we would meet to pray, read the Bible, and socialize together. Having close friends who shared my faith encouraged me tremendously. Our group was called Umucyo Fellowship, which means "The Light Fellowship." We mentored younger students at school and in our church. Having lost my parents at such a young age, I was able to speak persuasively to them about the importance of loving and respecting their parents, especially during the rebellious adolescent years. "Don't take your parents for granted," I would say. "You will miss them terribly when they are gone. Honor and obey them now." Although I did not realize it at the time, I had begun to work in my Holy Father's "business."

After I graduated from high school in 2001, I was unclear about my next steps. In an effort to find direction, I decided to spend time with a Rwandan couple with whom I had cultivated a deep friendship in the preceding years. Festus and Veneranda were Anglican priests who lived in a suburb of Nairobi called Karen. Before leaving Rwanda for Kenya, both had become good friends with my parents, and so they developed a special bond with me.

I had spent weekends with Festus and Veneranda during my time as a high school student in Kenya and had enjoyed relaxing and visiting with them in their large and comfortable home. But when I contacted them several months after leaving high school, I asked if I could come to their house for a specific purpose: I wanted to fast and pray for direction in my life. As I had expected, they welcomed me warmly, insisting that I stay for as long as I wanted. Their home was quiet and secluded and would provide the space and solitude I needed to hear from Jesus on this most important matter.

On the first day, at my request, they left me entirely alone and brought nothing but warm water to my room for me to drink. On the second day, they did the same. By the end of my second day of fasting and praying, the Holy Spirit spoke to me, not audibly, but through my mind: *Go for training. I want to use you.* I wrote what I had heard in my spirit on a piece of paper that I took to Festus and Veneranda the next morning at breakfast. "What does this mean?" I asked them.

They both laughed. "God wants you to go to seminary," Festus said with confidence. I had never even heard the word *seminary* before and had no idea what it meant. Festus explained it to me, and as he spoke, I felt excitement stir within my heart.

By the end of that week, I had decided to apply to seminary, and Festus and Veneranda agreed to assist me in identifying a list of possible schools. Given that my home church at that time was called Nairobi Pentecostal Church, they suggested I focus on those schools that prepared pastors for ministry in Pentecostal churches. Soon after, when my pastor learned of my intention to go to seminary, he narrowed the list to one school only: Pan Africa Christian College. "That's where I studied," he explained. "It will be perfect for you too." Festus and Veneranda agreed with my pastor, and I decided to follow their guidance. Together, we completed and submitted the application. Within a few short months, I received the good news. Not only had I been admitted to the college, but at age twenty-one, I was the youngest person ever admitted as a degree candidate.

It was only after the celebration surrounding my acceptance to Bible college had subsided that reality dawned on me. How was I to pay for college? Following my high school graduation, Mr. Patrick had again invited me to return to Rwanda to live with his family, but I had declined his invitation. I had firmly made up my mind to remain in Kenya. He had also indicated that he could not continue to pay my rent and financially support me in Kenya indefinitely. His other children had moved on, some to Europe and others to different cities in Africa. I was the only one who remained at the house where I had lived for the past four years. He expected me to become more self-sufficient now that I had finished my secondary schooling. I agreed that this was a reasonable expectation. Mr. Patrick had already done so very much for me, I could not in good conscience ask him to pay for my college education as well.

The way in which Jesus paved the way for me to attend and eventually graduate from Bible college, debt-free, when I did not even have a job, still amazes me today. Money and other resources started trickling in from various unexpected sources during my first year. Eventually that trickle turned into a steady flow that covered my every need. Here is how it unfolded.

I first approached the president of the college and told him my predicament. He was sympathetic but had no scholarships to offer. "I am sorry, Bosco, but you need money as well as faith to attend Bible college," he said. "But if you can bring me even a small down payment on your bill, I will allow you to begin." This was itself a miracle. The paperwork from the college had indicated that students would need to pay their full annual tuition and fees in advance, prior to being allowed to start class. I, however, had been exempted from this requirement.

My next step was to go to the Bible Society of Kenya to inquire about the availability of a scholarship. I told my story to the front desk manager, and although she was extremely moved by my testimony, she informed me that the Bible Society was unable to help fund my studies. But this woman, whose name was Karen, wanted to help. "I do not have very much money," she said, "but I can help you in another way. Come back here tomorrow afternoon to see me."

The next day I returned, and to my surprise, she presented me with several large bags of clothes. "You and my husband are the same size, and he has a lot of really nice clothes that he does not wear. These are all for you." Inside was an assortment of shirts, pants, suits, ties, and even shoes that fit me perfectly. I stared at her with my mouth wide open, unable to say a word. Laughing, she continued, "My husband is currently on a missions trip in Australia. He will be happy to know that he could help support you in this way."

My friendship with Karen and her husband continued throughout my time in college. Periodically she would give me a few shillings, but it was her prayers, especially before exams, and her consistent words of encouragement that meant the most to me. "You will graduate, Bosco," she would tell me repeatedly. In the months and years that followed, I remember, the other students would often comment on my appearance. "You must have a wealthy sponsor," they would say. "You are always dressed so nicely." I would simply smile, knowing that Karen was indeed "wealthy," but not in the way they imagined.

But what initially opened the door to college during my first year was not the nice clothes; it was the one hundred pounds I received from England just days before classes were to begin. Although it was a mere fraction of my total bill, it was enough for the president of the college to allow me to start classes. "You must pay the entire bill by the end of the term," he firmly reminded me. The money had come in response to a letter I had written weeks before to a man who had lived on our street in Kigali and whom I had known since I was a child. I had learned he was living in England and written him to ask if he could assist me financially with my tuition. He responded by sending the money, but strangely he included no written communication whatsoever. In fact, after he sent the money, I never heard from him again. But that one-time gift was enough. It was the first "trickle" of assistance, and it was perfectly timed.

As the weeks passed, I would periodically receive small financial gifts from Festus and Veneranda, as well as Karen. Every shilling I received I gave to the college, no matter how small the amount. And these amounts were indeed small—more like a drip than a trickle. But I did not give up hope. Rather, I studied hard and refused to be distracted by the fact that I was in a very precarious financial position.

Just before the end of my first term, I attended a large Christian conference where I met a group of Nigerians who managed and operated a nonprofit organization that was based in the United Kingdom. Among their organization's initiatives was a charity that financially supported students attending postsecondary institutions. After I spoke at length with one of the senior members of the organization about my situation, he encouraged me to apply for one of their scholarships. I did so as soon as I returned to campus and then prayed daily for a positive response.

Not long after, I received news that I had been awarded a

scholarship that would cover the remaining expenses for my first year of college. I raced to the president's office, clutching the letter in hand. "My bill will be paid in full," I shouted as I waved the document in my hand.

To my surprise, the president was not as excited about the news as I had thought he would be. "Let's hold our celebration until the check actually arrives," he said with a hint of skepticism in his voice.

Time passed, and the promised check did not arrive at the appointed time. Every day I would rush to check my mailbox, but there was nothing. Fortunately for me, the president still allowed me to take my final exams even though I had an outstanding balance. But I knew, without even asking, that he would not allow me to start the next term unless my bill was paid. He had already bent the rules in my favor, more than he had for any other student, but he had reached his limit. All I could do was wait and pray.

Weeks later the president summoned me to his office. I was nervous. This was it. I was certain he was going to ask me to pack my things and leave campus. But when I entered his office, he greeted me with a smile and words I would never forget: "Go and praise God!" I was puzzled.

"What has happened?" I asked.

Reaching into his drawer, he pulled out an envelope. "Your check has finally arrived."

I reached for it to examine it more closely and was surprised to see the amount printed on the front. Not only was it enough to cover the balance I still owed for tuition, room, and board, there would even be a little left over for me to use for personal spending. I slowly sank into the nearest chair. "What happened?" I asked. "Why did it take so long to get here?"

The president explained that weeks ago he had decided to reach out to the charity himself to find out what was going on. It was a good thing he did. The charity told him that they had already mailed the check and had assumed I had received it since it had been cashed. The president's call prompted an internal inquiry, and the charity subsequently discovered that a rogue employee had stolen the check and had not mailed it as directed. The officials apologized profusely and promptly sent a replacement check, which had arrived that afternoon. "And there is one additional detail they had neglected to tell you. The scholarship is renewable!" The president could barely contain his excitement as he spoke. "It will be awarded to you every year until you graduate."

During each of my remaining years in college, I received enough money to meet my needs. In addition to the scholarship from the Nigerian charity, I got a dishwashing job on campus, which reduced my tuition fees. Another missionary couple also decided to join Karen, Festus, and Veneranda in providing periodic financial gifts, which helped cover my personal expenses. My church, which is now known as Christ Is The Answer Ministry (CITAM), also proved to be an important source of financial support during my final year of study. Without a doubt, the favor of God was upon me during my college years.

I graduated from Pan Africa Christian College in July 2005 and was hired a few months later, in October, to join the pastoral staff at a newly established branch of my church, CITAM Buruburu. This new campus was located on the east side of Nairobi and had been established in response to the tremendous growth of the main CITAM church in recent years. Buruburu received new attendees and the overflow from CITAM's main church on Valley Road. The congregation at Buruburu met in a spacious tent that had been set up in the middle of a large field and was capable of accommodating two thousand people.

It was there at Buruburu, where I worked as the youth pastor for five years, that I finally began to fulfill the promise I had made eight years earlier in Kakuma and again in the prison in Nairobi. I had promised Jesus I would serve him, and after I completed high school, he responded by telling me to get trained so he could use me. He then provided every resource necessary for me to complete the training he required. But the latter should not have surprised me. He had already saved me from genocide, bullets and grenades, swirling river water, disease, starvation, war, suicidal thoughts, refugee camps, and prison.

In light of all that had transpired, I was extremely grateful but not at all surprised that my college costs were paid in full. My faith had flourished due to these past experiences, and I knew by then that Jesus was capable of doing anything that he willed for me. Having lived through all of the trials I experienced from 1994 to 1997, I eagerly embraced the honor and privilege of being used by the One who had kept me for his purpose through those tumultuous years. Now, as a young pastor, all I wanted to do was to tell everyone who would listen about his astonishing goodness, mercy, and grace.

Epilogue

I n December 2001, shortly after completing my first term of Bible college, I returned to Rwanda. It was my first visit since 1994, and I had not wanted to go. I went only because the college administrator required that I submit several documents, including a copy of my birth certificate, in order to continue my studies. These documents were all in government offices in Kigali.

In the weeks prior to the trip, I discussed the matter with an older Rwandan woman, Miss Vestine, who worked at the Red Cross in Nairobi. I had become friends with her because she had adopted a young girl from a family that I had known when I was a child. During one of my many visits to their home, I told Miss Vestine that I needed to return to Rwanda but was very reluctant to go. I expressed my concerns, which included the fact that I did not have a place to stay, to her. "And I don't have enough money to stay in a hotel," I added.

Miss Vestine smiled. "You know, I may be able to help. I have to travel to Rwanda to get a new passport. Maybe I can schedule my trip for the same time that you will be going, and we can travel together. I have friends in Kigali who will be able to accommodate us both at their home." Weeks later Miss Vestine and I traveled for twenty-four hours, by bus, from Nairobi, via Kampala, to Kigali.

Entering Rwanda for the first time was difficult for me. But I had anticipated that it would be hard and had fortified myself with prayer in the days leading up to the trip. The very last thing I wanted to happen was for me to break down. While it was indeed an intensely emotional experience, I did not lose control. Not when we drove over the mountain I had climbed on my way to Ruhengeri after fleeing Kigali. Not when we passed the river I had been so afraid to cross. Not when we drove through the intersection where one member of the Interahamwe had tried to shoot me while another member of that same militia protected me. Not even when we drove by the very spot where grenades had exploded in front of the car in which I had been traveling as I tried to reach my parents in Gitamara. My entire body shook, and tears burned the back of my eyes. But I did not crumble. I was upheld by the mighty hand of God.

My trip to Rwanda lasted seven days. The pastor with whom Miss Vestine and I stayed worked for the Bible League, and he and his entire family welcomed us warmly. We became close friends, and I have stayed with them repeatedly on many of my subsequent visits to Rwanda. During that very first visit, they were extremely helpful. With their guidance, I was able to get the documents I needed from the various government agencies within the time allotted for our visit, which was no small feat. However, there was little time for anything else.

I chose not to visit my old neighborhood. It was still too soon for me. And I did not visit the Patrick family because the drive would have taken more time than I could spare. Visiting my extended family was also out of the question—I could not even remember the names of the villages where they lived. Nor did I try to find or visit anyone else in Kigali whom I remembered from my childhood. Reconnecting with people from my past was not the purpose of that first visit. It would have been too unpredictable and too draining. What would we have talked about anyway? My family? The genocide? No. I did not want to discuss any of these topics, so I decided it was best to not reach out to anyone.

The most positive thing to come from that first trip and the many other trips to Kigali that I have taken over the years was the realization that I have learned to forgive those who hurt me and killed my family. Anger no longer boils within me when I interact with my fellow Rwandans, and I am no longer ashamed to call myself Rwandan. Only Jesus could have accomplished that kind of transformation within me.

As I have interacted with Rwandans at home and abroad, however, I have discovered just how many still struggle with these issues so many years after the genocide. Because forgiveness remains elusive and anger still rears its ugly head periodically, it is impossible for complete personal and therefore national healing to occur. And so now and in the years to come, I look forward to fulfilling my promise to serve the Lord by inviting Rwandans and people from every nation who struggle with anger and unforgiveness to draw near to Christ. He requires us to forgive, and he provides the power for us to do so. He does not require anything of us that he is not able and willing to help us accomplish.

Whether you feel guilty because you are still angry and unable to forgive or because you have committed an awful wrong against another, draw near. Ask Christ to transform your mind and heart. Approach him in humility and readily relinquish your shame or your "right" to be angry. Replace it with obedience to the One who has already forgiven our wrongdoings and has promised us eternal life.

Regardless of what we have done or what someone has done to us, we should be assured that with Christ, we *all* get to start over fresh.

There is no action so horrific or emotion so bitter that it is beyond his reach. He will forgive, and he will equip us to do the same. If we just invite him to live and reign in our hearts, our individual slates will be wiped clean because "anyone who belongs to Christ has become a new person. The old life is gone; a new life has begun."[1]

Acknowledgements

M any people have helped to make this memoir possible, including the numerous "angels along the way" who helped to ensure my survival during that traumatic and tumultuous period of my life between 1994 and 1997. The depth of my gratitude for each of you is immeasurable.

To my Christ Is The Answer Ministries (CITAM) church family, friends, and colleagues who urged me for many years to write my story, thank you for your prayers and encouragement. You inspired me to finally get it done.

To my collaborator on this project, Karen Panton WalkingEagle, I am so grateful for your probing questions during our lengthy interviews, and your commitment to this project. You gently guided me to recall memories I thought I had forgotten, and helped me to accurately and creatively portray the emotional truth of my experiences.

To Richard Stearns, I have always been inspired by your tremendous work on behalf of impoverished children worldwide, and I am honored that you graciously agreed to write such an insightful and thought-provoking foreword to my story. Your contribution to this work is invaluable and so appreciated.

To the editors at Havendale Press, Rosemarie Robotham-Arrindell and Paula Kay Panton, thank you for your care and expertise. Your attentive reading through several rounds of this manuscript sensitively enhanced the narrative. And to Cathy Richmond Robinson, who designed the beautiful cover and interior pages, thank you for lending your creativity and technical skills to this project.

Finally, my deepest love and gratitude to my wife, Everlyn, and our children, Isabellah and Ivan, whose love and support mean more to me that I can possibly express. I thank the Lord for blessing me with each of you, every day.

Notes

Chapter 11   The Four Laws
1   https://knowgod.com/en/fourlaws.
2   Mark 8:22–26 (NLT).

Chapter 12   A New Beginning
1   Deuteronomy 31:6 (NLT).
2   Philippians 4:4 (NLT).

Chapter 15   Angel along the Way
1   Proverbs 3:5–6 (NLT).
2   Hebrews 13:2 (NLT).

Chapter 16   Miracles
1   Philippians 4:7 (NLT).

Chapter 18   Destiny Revealed
1   Isaiah 55:8 (NLT).

Epilogue
1   2 Corinthians 5:17 (NLT).

About the Authors

Reverend Jean Bosco is an ordained minister with Christ Is The Answer Ministries (CITAM), which serves congregations in Kenya, Namibia, Romania, East Timor, and the United States. Together with his wife, Everlyn, he works to strengthen marriages and prepare the next generation for service through the teaching of biblical truth. Reverend Bosco preaches to approximately fifteen hundred people weekly, both online and in person, and he is frequently invited to address thousands more at conferences and seminars in the United States and Africa. A graduate of Pan Africa Christian University in Kenya, Reverend Bosco lives in Maryland with Everlyn and their children. *Kept for a Purpose* is his first book. Reverend Bosco is available for speaking engagements and can be contacted via email at j79bosco@gmail.com. Follow him on Twitter @RevBosco.

Karen Panton WalkingEagle is an attorney, author, and former high school teacher. Her first book, *BLESS*, was published in 2017. Her third book, a Bible study based on true stories from the international work of the Ageno Foundation, is scheduled to be released in 2022. Ms. WalkingEagle lives in Fairfax, Virginia, with her husband, Rusty, and their sons. Ms. WalkingEagle can be contacted via email at info@havendalepress.com.

Made in the USA
Middletown, DE
03 June 2022

66636601R00137